STRONG WOMEN, STRONG LOVE

The Missing Manual for the Modern Marriage

Poonam Sharma, Ph.D.

www.StrongWomenStrongLove.com

COPYRIGHT AND DISCLAIMER

IMPORTANT NOTE: The approach in this book assumes that you are in a generally healthy relationship. If you are in a relationship that is unhealthy or abusive in nature, it is strongly recommended you seek professional mental health services.

This book is intended for informational and educational purposes only. It is not a substitute for consultation with a mental health professional and should not be construed as a form of, or substitute for counseling, psychotherapy, or other psychological service.

Table of Contents

Preface

*Being loved deeply by someone
 gives you strength,
while loving someone deeply
gives you courage.*
~Lao Tzu

My parents had never met each other before getting married in 1959. They were both in their early 20's when their families arranged their marriage in India. When my father recalls that day, he always notes that my mother's face was veiled, so he was not even sure who he was marrying! Over 50 years later, they remain married, as have most of their peers whose marriages were also arranged. Their generation rarely contemplated divorce because the reasons for marriage were more practical ones, and the stigma around divorce was tremendous.

1

Like many of you, it is hard for me to imagine myself agreeing to an arranged marriage. Having grown up in England and the United States, my ideas of marriage revolve around the typical story of meeting someone, falling in love, and getting married. That was the path I followed to marry my own husband over 15 years ago. Like many couples in the United States, our expectations of marriage have been largely centered on pursuing shared goals and meeting each other's emotional needs.

As society changes, so does the institution of marriage. In places, like India, that have historically embraced arranged marriages, this tradition is simply less necessary now because economic stability is no longer as dependent on practical alliances between families. So, marriage in India is now a hybrid of the arranged marriage and "love marriage." The new norm is that families introduce a couple to one another, but then only move forward with marriage if both individuals fully consent.

The Industrial Revolution, two world wars, Women's Movement, and sexual revolution reshaped modern life and relationships between men and women in the United States and other countries. In an increasingly isolated, mobile, capitalistic society, marriage is supposed to be a lifelong partnership that is a steady source of companionship, passion, and romance. Books about marriage reflect this fact. Most focus on improving the quality of the relationship between partners, examining who did what and whether it was right or wrong. There is very little discussion of how the social environment in which the relationship exists affects it.

As someone who has lived most of my life in the space between two vastly different cultures, one inside the home and one outside, I am always acutely aware of how much the social backdrop influences how people behave. Pressures and expectations vary from culture to culture, so what is considered normal in one society, may not be so typical in another. Unless you have a basis for comparison, it is challenging to determine which of your relationship difficulties are common and stem from the environment you live in, and how many are actually unique to the two of you. One consequence of not looking at the social context in which a relationship occurs is that people often misunderstand the source of difficulty in their marriage, defaulting to assuming that their partner is to blame for the problems in the relationship, when the real source could actually be social.

Making a marriage strong is no easy feat these days, as it requires, not only a clear understanding of the inner workings of a healthy relationship, but also a keen attunement to the environmental forces that can potentially wreak havoc on a marriage. With knowledge at both these levels, it becomes possible to nurture and shelter a marriage into a strong, satisfying relationship that withstands the test of time.

Introduction

Emotional strength develops
out of your openness and willingness
to tolerate, face, bear, and know
as much of your moment-to-moment
experience as possible.
Being vulnerable, fully present,
authentic, and genuine.
Living your truth.
~Joan Rosenberg, Ph.D.

This book is a guide to the simplest and most powerful means for increasing understanding, love, and passion in a marriage. Although anyone can benefit from the general concepts here, the primary audience is strong women in heterosexual relationships. Strong women value authenticity, personal growth, and genuine relationships. They are courageous and willing to embrace the truth, even if doing so causes some discomfort. Strong women are deeply committed to keeping both themselves and their relationships healthy and vibrant.

Strong women come from all walks of life. She may be the CEO of a major corporation, juggling tremendous work and family responsibilities. Or, she could be a busy, stay-at-home mom who is deeply invested in helping her children become successful, compassionate adults with good character. A strong woman could even be someone whose quiet, steady presence is a source of strength and inspiration to those around her.

Even the strongest women sometimes struggle in their marriages. Some of you may be so overloaded, trapped, and lost in all the demands on you, that prioritizing your marriage seems nearly impossible. Others of you, especially those accustomed to being in leadership roles at work, may find that your typical take-charge attitude is not always so well-received at home. The goal of this book is to help you identify common relationship traps and empower you to make real choices about who you want to be and the type of relationship you want to create.

The book is divided into five parts:

Part 1 is a discussion of how high levels of chronic stress and new expectations of men, women, and marriage challenge modern relationships.

Part 2 explores the powerful mindset and skills necessary to be a stronger woman and marriage partner.

Part 3 examines the specific behaviors that are well-known to damage relationships. Special attention is paid to conflict because managing it well is a vital key to relationship success.

Part 4 reveals the habits that keep love strong, as well as the strategies for sustaining emotional intimacy and passion over the long run.

Part 5 identifies powerful strategies for protecting your marriage from persistent, outside forces that threaten your relationship.

Most busy women don't have time to sift through mounds of relationship advice. This book presents important, practical material in a highly understandable, to-the-point format. You have easy access to the core relationship ideas and skills that clinicians and academics have identified as vital to keeping marriage strong.   The practical suggestions offered here are ones you can immediately apply.

Think of this book as a relationship manual you can refer to again and again.   In every chapter, you will find practical advice to help you strengthen your marriage.   As you review the information, it may be useful to keep a notebook handy to jot down ideas you would like to try in your personal life.   Each chapter ends with a "Bottom Line," a concise summary of the chapter's most important point.   For your convenience, a complete list of these main points is provided in Appendix A.

I'm excited you have decided to embark on this journey.   As I tell many of my own clients, it is the smartest and strongest people who seek out information and help when faced with adversity. As you move through the book, you may discover that you need to radically alter the way you have been approaching your relationship, or you may feel relieved that you are already largely on track.   My hope is that the information you find in this book helps you become more effective and confident in navigating relationship challenges and avoiding painful, unnecessary mistakes.

PART 1

IT'S NOT ALL YOU!

Why are so many competent women like you struggling with their marriages? Is it that you don't know what you are doing, or is there something bigger going on, perhaps? Part 1 takes a closer look at the social factors that influence our relationships and make them more challenging to navigate these days. Understanding this backdrop is critical to figuring out how you can begin to deal with any relationship problems you face.

1

YES, MARRIAGE THESE DAYS REALLY IS CONFUSING!

Unfortunately, a marriage license doesn't come with a job description or a set of instructions. There is definitely "some assembly required." In fact, putting together a modern-day marriage can be likened to assembling an airplane in flight.
~Dr. Patricia Love

In my work as a psychologist, I have encountered many women struggling with relationships and have witnessed the same pattern over and over. A woman meets a fabulous guy. They fall in love and get married. Things are great...for a while. And then, the decline begins. They start arguing more often and feel less connected. If they have children, things worsen more quickly. In the end, so many wonder, "How did I get here?" Some even reach out to their friends to get help with their marital problems, but find their friends are typically not faring much better. Everyone is "working" on their marriage, but in the end, most either assume incorrectly that misery is just the reality of marriage, or they divorce. Very few find another solution.

It is difficult to grapple with relationship problems when life is moving at a frantic pace. Women these days are busier than ever. We are attempting to excel in challenging careers, keep the love in our marriages alive, and nurture our children. Days are intense and full of pressure, overflowing with deadlines at work, after-school activities, bedtime routines, housework, meal preparation, office meetings, and the list goes on. It is easy to get tired and disillusioned in the process of attempting to meet all these demands. No doubt, there is a heavy cost to pursuing so many goals at the same time, without any breathing room to even consider the "big picture."

When life is moving so rapidly, it becomes very hard to stay focused on what you value most. Especially after having children, it's easy to become disconnected from yourself, forgetting who you are, what you need, and what stirs your passion in life. Your marriage can be another casualty if the close connection with your husband erodes into two strangers sharing household tasks, living parallel lives, without much intimacy at all. Over time, such distance can seem unbridgeable.

Common complaints men and women have of one another

Within the walls of my office, I hear women express many complaints about their mates. See if any of them seem familiar to you:

- I wish I could get him to change.
- He doesn't listen.
- He never talks to me. I don't think he cares about me anymore.
- I feel so alone in this relationship.
- He doesn't help around the house. I gave him a list of things to do, and he still has not done them. Why can't he see I need help?
- He only pays attention to me when he wants to have sex.
- Even when he's home, it's like he's not there. He's just focused on himself and ignores me.
- When we argue, he won't work things out. He runs off, pretending nothing is happening.

- He hardly ever calls me to see how I'm doing.
- He's obsessed with work and doesn't seem to care about anything else.
- I do five million things every day, and he doesn't even appreciate my efforts.
- He doesn't say he's sorry, even when he hurts my feelings.
- He actually forgot my birthday this year.
- He just doesn't care about me anymore.

Husbands are not faring much better. Their experiences are a little different, but they are just as frustrated as their wives. Men often complain that their wives criticize them constantly, try to change them, and micromanage everything they do. They often feel unappreciated, misunderstood, and cast aside when their wives become extremely busy, especially after having children. Many men are unclear about how to make their wives happy, so they assume a resigned stance in the marriage in response to these feelings of powerlessness.

Yes, relationships can truly be challenging. People demand much more of their marriages now than in the past, and if relationships do not live up to these hopes and dreams, divorce is often seen as a viable option. The divorce rate remains high, and most divorces are now initiated by women. However, the remarriage rate is also high, indicating people have not given up on marriage entirely, but feel they simply chose the wrong partner. Unfortunately, second marriages have an even higher divorce rate than the first, and the rate climbs further for a third marriage. If the selection of the wrong mate is the primary reason for marital problems, why do the statistics tell such a different story?

I do believe it is possible to marry the wrong person and that there are legitimate reasons for leaving a marriage. Sometimes people *do* marry too young or end up with someone who is incapable of having a healthy relationship. Or, a marriage may need to end because there's simply too much water under the bridge, and the relationship is beyond repair. However, it is curious that so many competent, resourceful, strong women *and* men are reporting the *same* relationship problems. I don't think it is any coincidence that the same patterns are seen among so many marriages.

The issue is NOT that people don't care about one another. The problem is that caring is not enough to keep love strong. Navigating a relationship has become more complex in modern times. When marital difficulties inevitably arise, most people don't know what to do and are simply too busy to figure it out, so they fly by the seat of their pants. This is especially true of professional women whose lives have become increasingly pressured by juggling multiple roles in the pursuit of their dreams. The remarkable change in men's and women's roles over the past few decades adds even more confusion to the mix.

Without a solid understanding of how to keep a relationship healthy AND a clear mindset capable of defeating the unrelenting forces that threaten a marriage, even the best romantic pairing may not survive.

Is there hope?

Despite the long list of problems people describe, couples *can* build a marriage satisfying to both parties. If you and your husband are generally mature individuals who are even a little open to trying, I am incredibly optimistic that you can turn around a struggling relationship. However, it is vital to make changes before negativity floods the relationship, and it is too late.

Dump the bad relationship advice, and discover what really works.

In the course of writing this book, I reviewed many of the most popular relationship resources out there. Some of them are helpful, but the majority of them, unfortunately, perpetuate misinformation about men, women, and how relationships work, including the following:

- If you're lucky enough to find the right guy, you will have a happy marriage.
- Women are more emotional than men.
- Conflict is bad for a relationship.
- Men are generally selfish and don't want to work on relationships.
- Men only care about a woman's looks, so focus on being physically attractive to keep him.
- Men are starved for sex and cannot control themselves.

There is a huge industry perpetuating some of these myths. It's big business helping women figure out how to "hook" a man, become "magnetic" to him, and lure him like a "siren" to be "irresistible" to him forever. The goal of companies that promote these ideas is to make money, not disseminate accurate relationship advice! Here are some suggestions you've probably heard that are disrespectful, harmful, or just plain unrealistic:

- Play hard to get. Show interest in him and then back off. Be unpredictable. Keep him confused so he doesn't get bored with you. (Even if this does work, who has the time to implement this strategy?)

- You need to remain sexually seductive at all times or a man will fall out of love with you. (Good luck, you sleep-deprived moms of newborns!)
- Don't be too nice to him. Being a little cruel helps him stay interested. (This is healthy?)
- Don't make any demands of him. (This is obviously a recipe for resentment on the woman's side.)
- The best way to get to a man is through his stomach. (Who knew that beer and barbeque were the secret ingredients for a strong marriage?)

The big problem with much of this advice (besides that fact that it is inaccurate!) is that it comes from a very narrow approach based on fear. It leaves the impression that if you don't do just the right thing at just the right time, there goes your relationship. A fear-based approach in a relationship assumes that the other person has little capacity to trust, commit, or engage in a mature, responsible way. Is this really the mindset you want to have in your marriage?

Fear-based approaches to love do not work in the long run. A person stays in a relationship because of how their partner makes them feel about themselves and how well that relationship meets their needs. If you want to keep your love strong, you must step into a place of COURAGE- the courage to be honest, to love deeply, and to live your life to the fullest. Courage is the leap of faith you take AFTER you have done your homework!

Fortunately, the leap of faith is not huge. There is plenty of knowledge in academic and professional circles about sustaining a healthy relationship. Some of this information makes it to the media, but most of it does not. This book is your bridge to some of the most important information we know about making love last.

BOTTOM LINE

The modern environment makes it harder to navigate a relationship.

The social environment perpetuates fear, confusion, and bad advice about relationships. You must develop a solid understanding of how to keep a relationship healthy and maintain a courageous mindset capable of defeating the unrelenting forces that threaten a marriage.

2

IF THE RULES OF MARRIAGE HAVE CHANGED, WHERE'S THE REVISED MANUAL?

Nobody will ever win
the Battle of the Sexes.
There's just too much
fraternizing with the enemy.
~Henry Kissinger

Social expectations of marriage have changed considerably in recent history, as marriage has evolved from a practical arrangement for economic security to a union of soul mates. A spouse is now asked to meet a tremendously-wide range of needs, without consideration for whether that individual has the capacity to do so. Men have pressure to be more emotionally open, participate in child rearing, and fully share household tasks, even though the upbringing of most American boys still emphasizes competence over connection and provides limited exposure to domestic chores and child care. The extension of women's roles into arenas that were previously the exclusive domain of men, such as providing financially for the family, also has many men confused about what being a man means these days.

All these unrealistic demands can make marriage highly stressful. Although it is simply impossible for one person to be everything for another, the pressure is still on married people to try. Many women now expect their husbands to be strong, competitive, and tough in the outside world, but also sensitive, cooperative, and emotionally vulnerable at home. Men often assume their wives will effortlessly manage the responsibilities of work, home, and social life, while also maintaining their physical and sexual appeal. Inevitably, both men and women experience genuine disappointment in their partners when they fall short of these expectations.

Hidden assumptions and expectations about gender roles often strain the relationship between the sexes. Here are some common situations that often baffle women as they relate to men. See if you have ever experienced any of the following scenarios in your personal life:

- You sit on the couch next to your spouse watching a football game all evening. You complain that the two of you never "connect." He says, "What are you talking about? We just spent all this time together!"
- Your husband's mother just died. You gently ask him if he's okay and he says, "I'm fine," and then never seems willing to talk about it again.
- You're really upset about a hurtful comment a friend made and tell your husband about it. He advises you to confront your friend or let go of it. When you continue to share more details about what happened, he seems impatient, until you finally say, "Just forget it!" and storm out.
- You're having an argument with your spouse and honestly reveal all the reasons why you are feeling resentful toward him. He sits in complete silence, never responding to your comments.
- You have guests coming to stay in your home in one week and want your husband to mow

the grass and clean up the flower beds. You tell him you would like this done, help him by giving him your ideas for how to get this task completed on time, and periodically check in to make sure things are progressing. Two days before your guests arrive, you are livid because nothing has been done yet. You let him have it, telling him you're sick and tired of not being able to count on him and will just hire a landscaping service to do the work.

Men and women *can* have better relationships, but we need to start by critically examining the messages all of us have been given about what it means to be a man or woman in American society. This chapter sheds some light on the ways both sexes are socialized and how such experiences commonly affect how they behave in relationships. It offers effective relational strategies for reducing tension that arises from gender differences.

Are we from Mars, Venus, or Planet Earth?

The topic of differences between the sexes is highly complex and emotionally charged. Even in academic circles, people have very strong opinions about whether differences between men and women are biologically based or stem from learning. If you start exploring the possibility that one sex might be better at something than the other, things get heated even faster. John Gray, author of *Men are from Mars, Women are from Venus,* has been ostracized professionally for exaggerating sex differences, although he continues to be extremely popular with the public.

Please note that in this chapter, I speak in generalities, not because I think people fit into neat little boxes, but because boxes sometimes help us organize and understand information. I will be discussing the most common ways men and women behave, not the only ways. The research literature clearly shows that there are many more differences *within* groups of men and *within* groups of women than between the sexes, which is why it is inaccurate to say ALL women are like this or ALL men are like that. Remember that there is tremendous variability among people and that not everyone fits my descriptions (e.g., think of role reversals). Also, even if a person is born with certain natural tendencies, it does not mean that they cannot learn how to behave in new ways.

So, as we move forward, I encourage you to consider whether my descriptions fit your individual situation. Sweeping statements made about men or women may be highly inaccurate when applied to your partner because other factors, such as cultural upbringing, personality, or level of education also influence development. Details matter tremendously when relating effectively to the person you married.

Understanding how your partner learned to be a "real" man

Men are commonly exposed to some distinct messages about masculinity. Awareness of these messages can help you understand frequent ways men interact in relationships, thereby reducing your misinterpretation of their behavior in relationships.

According to psychologist Dr. William Pollack in *Real Boys: Rescuing Our Sons from the Myths of Boyhood,* males still clearly receive the message that they must *never* be perceived as weak. Pollack says the "Boy Code" essentially teaches them, "Be a man, be strong, be brave, don't be a sissy, don't show your feelings." In other words, don't ever show your vulnerability, and whatever you do, *never* be perceived as feminine. Think of how rare it is, even these days, to find a parent who is comfortable allowing their son to play with dolls, cry profusely when he is hurt, or tell everyone his favorite color is pink, and you can see how "The Boy Code" is still alive and well.

Although humans by nature are interdependent, men are asked to function in a largely self-sufficient manner. The traditional world of men is highly competitive, placing tremendous pressure on men to perform and appear strong at all times. Competence, emotional control, rationality, and the ability to overcome challenges independently are revered qualities. Expressing feelings, seeking reassurance, or acknowledging difficulty may be perceived as signs of weakness that place men at risk of being ridiculed, criticized, or shamed by others. The status of being a "real" man is something earned, not something given to a man simply by virtue of his sex. Men must demonstrate that they can hold their own to be respected by others.

Men who attempt to take on less traditional roles may experience considerable confusion and frustration. The expectation that a man provide financially for his family is still prevalent, and men are often judged negatively if they depend on their wives for financial support. Think of the challenge a full-time, stay-at-home-dad faces. Although society encourages him to be an involved, loving father, he is not considered to be a "real man" if being a full-time father interferes with his ability to bring home a paycheck.

Shame is a powerful tool used to socialize men into traditional roles. The normal human reaction to excessive shame is to pull away from others and hide vulnerability. Out of necessity, men frequently appear tough, and some of them have become so adept at walling off their emotions, that expressing feelings actually feels strange. Psychologist Dr. Ronald Levant notes that some men cannot even identify what they are feeling, something he calls "normative male alexithymia." All too often, men attempt to escape intense feelings through the use of alcohol or drugs, or they physically exit the situation generating strong emotions. Research shows that men tend to be much more emotionally isolated than women and have higher rates of suicide and chemical addiction.

The only emotion that men do *not* have to suppress is anger, as American society does not consider anger to be an indicator of weakness. From what I have seen, some men definitely have an intact ability to experience a wide range of emotions, but don't always feel safe enough in their relationships to do so. Even in a therapist's office, where one of the explicit goals is transparency, the vulnerability associated with such an endeavor can be disconcerting for many men.

Psychologist Dr. Roy Baumeister openly questions how "good" men really have it. In a 2007 speech to the American Psychological Association entitled "Is There Anything Good about Men?" Baumeister discusses both the social rewards and costs of being male and the dangers of assuming one sex always has it better than the other:

When I say I am researching how culture exploits men, the first reaction is usually "How can you say culture exploits men when men are in charge of everything?" ...The mistake in that way of thinking is to look only at the top. If one were to look downward to the bottom of society instead, one finds mostly men there too. Who's in prison, all over the world, as criminals or political prisoners? The population on Death Row has never approached 51% female. Who's homeless? Again, mostly men. Whom does society use for bad or dangerous jobs? U.S. Department of Labor statistics report that 93% of the people killed on the job are men.

The broader culture reinforces roadblocks to men's full engagement in relationships, by portraying them as immature, incompetent, and emotionally unaffected (i.e., think Homer Simpson, Al Bundy, or most men in sitcoms). No doubt, we have all heard that:

- Men are little boys.
- Men are unemotional.
- Men are clueless about women and children.
- Men have a one-track mind.

"Who needs a man? They are good for nothing" is a prevalent attitude. Sometimes people jokingly count the husband when tallying up how many children are in a family. Male bashing among female friends is even a legitimate form of bonding. Needless to say, all these ideas are ultimately destructive to intimacy in relationships because they erode respect and trust. Rather than create an environment that allows men to become more familiar with emotional intimacy, American society assumes men lack the innate capacity to relate well and promotes incredibly low standards for men in relationships.

What women unknowingly do that triggers most men to get defensive

The male mandate to conceal vulnerability often leads men to become highly defensive and uncomfortable when women push them to be more transparent and to engage at a more intimate level. When women openly point out mistakes in an attempt to be honest, men often get their feelings hurt and respond by becoming irritated or retreating into silence. Women often have no idea how sensitive and vulnerable men often are under the surface.

Because they are under constant social pressure to be competent and have all the answers, men often take complaints very personally. Psychologist Dr. David Wexler notes that relationships serve as a mirror, reflecting back how we are perceived by others. Many men fear looking in the mirror and seeing a highly flawed reflection. For most men, their partner is the most potent mirror, so feedback from her has the emotional capacity to injure him deeply. Men fear looking in the mirror and seeing an unhappy wife who sees him as weak and incapable.

Even if you are just trying to be "open" and let him know you have unmet needs, if he believes you are miserable, he may feel he has failed you. As corny as it may sound, he wants you to see him as a hero and needs to know he can make you happy. He has been taught to use your happiness as a measure of his success in a relationship, and much of what motivates him is the desire to meet your needs.

I can recall numerous marriage therapy sessions in which a wife attempted to build intimacy by disclosing all the ways her husband was not meeting her expectations, while he sat and listened in complete silence. From a male point of view, her publicly noting his weaknesses (and so many of them at once!) is an act of aggression and disrespect. His response of silence is simply an attempt to retreat from what he perceives as an "attack." Having seen this pattern many times, I often intervene quickly to move the couple into a more constructive stance by acknowledging both his position and positive intentions. I usually say something like:

I can see by the fact that you are here that you must love your wife deeply. You seem like a really competent, smart guy, but here's the deal: Most men are told they need to keep their wives happy, but are simply not given the tools to accomplish that. It takes guts to come in here and openly discuss the ways the two of you are struggling so that you can figure out how to make your marriage stronger. I really admire you for that. The good news is that you already have the most important part down—you care. All we are doing here is fine-tuning.

I find the average wife is surprised to learn her husband is actually upset when he is quiet because she was fooled by his appearing so emotionally composed. She is usually quite relieved that his behavior is not due to a lack of caring and approaches him with much more compassion and realistic expectations, once she understands what is happening. So, the lesson here is to be careful about assuming a man is emotionally unaffected just because you don't see an obvious display of feeling. There is still a human being on the inside who can be terribly hurt by cruel words, even if he has learned not to show it.

Given the tendency of most men to act tough, you may think that women love men who are actually comfortable with emotional expressiveness and vulnerability. Although the party line is that men should be more open, the response to such transparency is not always positive. Surprisingly, many women say they are turned off by a man who is "too feminine," and feel most attracted to the strength and confidence of a more dominant man. So, the double bind for men is that women may actually reject them if they seem too vulnerable. The current social environment is truly confusing for everyone.

What about you?
How much of a woman are you?

As women, we face our own fair share of pressure to conform to society's expectations of what constitutes a "real woman." Dr. Warren Farrell, author of *The Myth of Male Power*, points out that men are treated as "success objects," while women are often treated as "sex objects" by our society. The ideal woman is physically attractive, emotionally supportive, and a good listener. She can have a husband, children, and a career, but must successfully juggle all these roles, so no one is inconvenienced by her choices. A woman can do anything a man can do, but has subtle pressure to always be mindful of her partner's ego, making sure she is not too outspoken, competitive, or perceived as more successful than him. Society says a real woman is adaptable and eager to put the needs of others, especially her children, ahead of her own.

If her marriage is struggling, kids are misbehaving, or house is not well-kept, the woman will be judged, not her partner. Many high-achieving women fear falling short of social expectations and spend all their time trying to live up these unrealistic standards. This can cause considerable strain in a marriage, especially when her husband does not understand her pressures and may not be so "cooperative" when she asks for his help in achieving goals he considers unnecessary.

Tapping the power of diversity

In addition to individual expectations of men and women, there are also some new mandates for relationships. We have all been challenged to become more "equal" partners in our marriages. I personally believe that the term "equal" is often misunderstood in the context of relationships. There is an assumption that for a woman to be equal to a man, she must be just like him. Equal has become equated with "same." As a result, many women feel pressure to actively reject traditional feminine ideals such as being sensitive, accommodating, or gentle in favor of traditional male qualities like independence, dominance, and competitiveness, especially since these behaviors are revered in the workplace. Women were historically trapped by the expectations of traditional femininity; now, they are often bound by the pressure to be more like men. In the end, most people are not exercising real choice about how they define themselves.

Equality in relationships is *not* about men and women having the exact same characteristics; it is about each individual having the same *worth*. We need to stop aiming to be cookie-cutter replicas of one another and embrace the differences that will inevitably exist between any two human beings, regardless of their sex. Diversity is strength. We need *all* the qualities human beings can express, from dominance to vulnerability or from independence to connection. The more diversity we embrace, the greater flexibility and choice we *all* have in defining ourselves. Having a range of ways we can respond increases our effectiveness in relationships.

Protecting your marriage from gender expectations

In the midst of all the changes in men's and women's roles, what I see in my office is increased fear, competition, and confusion in relationships. Couples are often lost in power struggles, aggressively vying for control and demanding love in an attempt to get their needs met. Insecurity is prevalent, while deep trust is conspicuously missing. Loneliness and a sense of failure exist on both sides of the relationship.

Women hoping to successfully engage men must remember that underneath the composed exterior of any person is the vulnerability that is simply part of being human. *Everyone* fears being judged when they let the world see who they truly are underneath that layer of protection. Because of socialization, the stakes may be higher for men, yet the most emotionally-rich marriages are ones where it is safe for *both* men and women to be real with one another.

If you seek to improve your marriage, I challenge you to keep your own ego in check and to draw on traditional feminine qualities, such as gentleness and emotional sensitivity to approach your husband. For him to fully engage, he needs to feel you believe in him, are generally happy, and want to improve the marriage, not place blame on him. Consider some of the following strategies for facilitating connection:

- **Assume the best.** Remember that at one point this was the man you loved enough to want a lifelong commitment. Start with the assumption that he loves you and look for common ground, responding kindly and generously whenever you can.
- **Embrace differences in styles of relating.** We all grew up hearing different messages about how we should relate, so don't assume that because your husband's style is different from yours, that it needs

"fixing." One approach is not "superior" to the other. Get curious and learn more about your individual styles. The larger the difference, the more open, respectful, and flexible both of you will need to be.

- **Turn complaints into requests and directly negotiate for what you need.** Minimize how much you complain and dare to directly ask for what you actually need from your husband. Remember that he wants you to be happy, but cannot read your mind. For example, instead of saying, "You don't love me anymore," try, "A big hug from you right now would really lift me up." If something feels unfair, negotiate with him to change that. If you are clear and motivated to create a win/win for both of you, he will be more responsive to you. So, instead of wishing he would help with the dishes, say, "I find it really helpful when we can share the task of washing dishes. How about we take turns every other day? That would really lift some stress off me."

- **Make sure there is space for him in your life.** As the list of responsibilities grows, it is all too easy to relegate your husband to the bottom of your "to do" list. Spending too little time with your husband, or engaging him only when you need help with other priorities can lead a man to feeling like he is only a means to an end, an observer in your life, or simply dispensable. It is important to convey how your husband's presence and actions add value and meaning to your life, and keep him high on the priority list.

- **Understand that his priorities and timelines may not be the same as yours.** Men face different pressures from women. This means you will need to be direct in helping him understand why something is SO important to you and why it needs to be done right now. Even then, remember that he is an adult and has the option to say "no" after you make your request.

To be clear, I am not suggesting that you abandon your own needs and absolve your husband of his responsibility to work with you to strengthen your marriage. Men are not children and should never be treated as such. I *am* encouraging you to factor in whether gender differences are possibly the reason behind some of the difficulties you may be experiencing in your marriage.

If you are seeking emotional intimacy and find yourself consistently running into barriers, you must realistically assess whether your partner will be able to meet your needs. If you are married to a man who has exhibited emotional vulnerability in the past, but has merely distanced from you, it may be possible to reengage him. If your spouse is the stoic cowboy type whose whole identity centers on this persona, you may need to readjust your expectations.

Being well-versed in the common pressures both men and women face puts you in the position of being able to develop more realistic expectations for deepening the emotional connection with your partner. As I said earlier, it helps if your default is to believe that your partner's intentions are positive, and that his love for you is real, especially when misunderstandings occur. I have personally witnessed hundreds of situations in which a woman assumed her partner was intentionally withholding what she needed, and it turned out he was just completely unaware and did not mean to upset or hurt her at all.

The larger the differences between you and your spouse, the more mindful you will need to be about potential miscommunication. When misunderstandings do occur, the same kindness and respect you would extend to a close friend become vital tools for preventing a rift from developing.

Men and women are much more alike than different inside. Anyone can appear invincible on the outside, but none of us, including men, are immune to the self-doubt or worry all human beings experience. These vulnerabilities are present within each of us and will either be revealed when communication is good, or hidden when it is not. So, be constructive on your end by treating your spouse with compassion, understanding, and respect. Always remember to clearly ask for what you need, and generously extend good will to each other.

BOTTOM LINE

All of us have a need to be understood, appreciated, and cherished.

Men and women may seem quite different from one another. Although there is much confusion about gender roles and whether men and women differ in their capacities for engagement at a more intimate level, remember that we are all human and have similar core emotional needs.

3

WE'RE DROWNING IN STRESS AND DRAGGING OUR RELATIONSHIPS DOWN WITH US.

Tension is who you
think you should be.
Relaxation is who you are.
~Chinese Proverb

Understanding how expectations of men, women, and marriage have changed enhances the ability to relate more effectively. It is also crucial to step back and take a look at the general health of the environment in which your marriage exists. This is akin to examining the water in which a goldfish swims to make sure there are not any pollutants that could harm it.

One obvious threat to relationships is the skyrocketing level of stress in our daily lives. Although human beings are wired for connection, stability, and operating within certain limits, in recent decades, the social pressure to ignore this biological reality has increased. As a result, high stress, which is detrimental to personal and relationship health, is running rampant. In this chapter, we will explore the nature of stress and how constant exposure to exorbitant levels of stress affects marriages, decreasing the likelihood that they will survive over the long run.

Be warned: A marriage under too much stress will fall apart.

Researchers Dr. Lisa Neff and Dr. Benjamin Karney suggest that relationships exposed to excessive stress will inevitably falter. Their research has demonstrated that marital partners enduring higher-than-normal levels of stress for extended periods tend to be much more reactive to the normal ups and downs of their relationships. This finding was even stronger for women. Studies also showed that under heavy stress, couples have more difficulty seeing the positive in their relationship and usually magnify anything negative that is happening. Unfortunately, because of the way the brain works, even if a person has excellent relationship and communication skills, it is very hard to draw on those skills when overwhelmed.

High levels of stress make you very reactive to anything coming at you because more primitive parts of the brain are engaged, literally making it difficult to think. So, you might respond a little too defensively to the "tone" in your partner's voice. And those dirty socks on the floor may throw you right over the edge! If you are in reactive mode, by definition, you are not making a real choice about how you want to respond.

What goes on inside you that makes it so hard to control yourself when you are stressed out? And how do you move into a position of making real choices, rather than just reacting all over the place? Let's take a closer look at the inner workings of the body's hardwired stress response, what fuels it, and how to tame it.

The hardwired response to threat

Stress is what you experience when there are physical or psychological demands on you. A small dose of stress can be stimulating. However, when you are exposed to high stress, your brain activates an automatic stress response called the "fight-or-flight response." This response is triggered by brain centers responsible for physical survival. When there is significant stress, the body quickly releases adrenaline and cortisol into your bloodstream. Blood pressure, heart rate, and respiration rise, while blood flows away from your hands and feet to your large muscles. From an evolutionary standpoint, the fight-or-flight response prepares your body to either escape from danger or face the threat. A caveman being pursued by a dangerous animal couldn't have survived without this response!

In our modern lives, we are exposed to stressful events all day long, and our brains have a difficult time distinguishing which of these events are genuinely threatening. For example, if you are crossing the street and a car almost hits you, a stress response would be activated because this is a real threat to your physical safety. However, if you are running late for an appointment, stuck in wall-to-wall traffic, or trying to meet a deadline at work, you might still activate the same stress response, but it would be a "false alarm." Some estimates indicate that, in a city the size of Boston, a person might engage the stress response over 50 times a day! How many times this week have you already noticed you are stressed and wished there was a way to escape?

Dangers of chronic stress on health

Persistent stress can wear on health. Stress can decrease the strength of your immune system, making you much more vulnerable to infections. Stress also leads to increased muscle tension, especially in the jaws, neck, shoulders, and lower back. Headaches, stomach problems, and palpitations can result from long-term exposure to stress.

From a psychological standpoint, chronic stress can lead to fear, anxiety, depression, and irritability. High stress typically also results in trouble sleeping, difficulty concentrating, and tunnel vision. As a result, distressed people often appear more controlling, rigid, and judgmental. All these things make it much harder to be an emotionally-available partner, so do ultimately affect the health of your marriage as well.

What keeps us trapped in stress?

Breaking out of the cycle of excessive stress can be difficult since the nature of our lifestyles supports its continuation. An important step in reducing stress is starting to become more aware of the circumstances that perpetuate it and taking small steps to push back against these factors. Let's review some common factors that exacerbate stress.

1. Your most basic needs are not being met.

The American Psychological Association's annual survey, *Stress in America,* continues to indicate, year after year, that one-quarter to one-third of Americans report extreme stress. The top sources of stress reported in 2011 were the following:

- Money (75%)
- Work (70%)
- Economy (67%)
- Relationships (58%)
- Family responsibilities (57%)
- Family health problems (53%)
- Personal health concerns (53%)
- Job stability (49%)
- Housing costs (49%)
- Personal safety (32%)

If you've ever taken a psychology class, you may remember learning about Abraham Maslow's Hierarchy of Needs. Maslow provided us with a list of the core needs of a human being, placing the most essential needs at the base of the hierarchy:

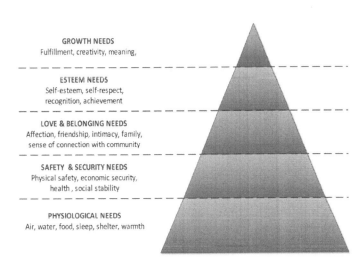

GROWTH NEEDS
Fulfillment, creativity, meaning,

ESTEEM NEEDS
Self-esteem, self-respect,
recognition, achievement

LOVE & BELONGING NEEDS
Affection, friendship, intimacy, family,
sense of connection with community

SAFETY & SECURITY NEEDS
Physical safety, economic security,
health , social stability

PHYSIOLOGICAL NEEDS
Air, water, food, sleep, shelter, warmth

Adaptation of Maslow's Hierarchy of Needs

If you compare the top sources of stress with the needs listed in the pyramid, you will see that most stress emerges from the struggle to meet basic human needs. Stress related to keeping a roof over your head, staying healthy, and maintaining decent relationships is what concerns most people.

When your needs are not met, you suffer. Sometimes it is your health that suffers. Other times it's the children. Much too often, it is the marriage. Reflect on the following questions to examine if excessive stress may be a problem you need to address in your life:

- How often do you skip meals or fail to drink enough water?
- Do you consider it normal to be chronically sleep-deprived?
- Are you resigned to only seeing your family for just a few minutes each day during the work week?
- How often do you bring your best self to your relationships?
- In what ways is the stress in your marriage intensified by the fact that your basic needs are not being met?

2. You believe that you are not enough and do not have enough.

Victoria Castle, in her book *The Trance of Scarcity: Stop Holding Your Breath and Start Living Your Life,* calls into question a central story most of us living in American culture have internalized:

> I am not enough
> There is never enough

I am not enough means that no matter what the reality, you always believe you are never smart enough, rich enough, beautiful enough, successful enough, etc. Because you are never good enough, you assume you must always struggle in order to achieve anything in life. You feel constantly pressured and are so physically tightly wound that even breathing in a relaxed manner becomes difficult.

There is never enough translates into the belief that no matter what you do, you will never have enough of what you need or want. The highly stressful search for *enough* money, time, love, success, is endless, and the sense of fear of never having enough of these things, profound. Constantly collecting material goods and fiercely protecting your gains are common outcomes of this assumption.

This story of scarcity constrains hope, reducing your capacity to feel you are good enough and to lead a fulfilling life. Castle argues that the Trance of Scarcity prevents you from expressing your natural greatness, creativity, caring, and resilience, moving you, instead, into a state of numbness and disconnection from your true self. Living in a constant state of deprivation generates tremendous stress.

3. You value work over everything else.

In a culture of scarcity, money and work become glorified, as they are the primary means for attaining material success. Work is clearly valued over relationships in the U.S., and this is ultimately not good for any of us. Most people are employed by companies that expect them to give a 150% and insist that other important priorities be kept separate from work. People are pushed to sacrifice their personal ties in order to move anywhere that the job opportunities are better. Companies increasingly want employees to be accessible 24/7.

With the advent of technology, the connection to work is difficult to suspend. In the past, you could count on job security as a reward for all this loyalty. Now, it is nearly impossible to find a job that is truly secure. Most people know that they are expendable and are constantly distressed, knowing they must always be prepared for the rug to be pulled out from underneath their lives. They do their best to demonstrate "value" to employers by being at their beck and call. Relationships are taking the brunt of the hit from the overvaluing of work above everything else.

4. You're lonely.

We know that positive connections with a spouse, friends, family, and coworkers help buffer stress and make life more enjoyable. Having a network of support eases the emotional and practical burden on marriages and families. Sadly, because our communities are breaking down, many people are struggling with loneliness. Books such as Robert Putman's *Bowling Alone* and John Cacioppos's *Loneliness: Human Nature and the Need for Social Connection* detail the problem of loneliness in America. The average adult in the U.S. has only two people they can talk to about the most important things in their lives, and one of them is probably their spouse. Times of transition or disruption make us most vulnerable to loneliness. Research shows that people aged 18 to 30 are the loneliest group in America, as that particular stage of life is full of change.

The pressure on our marriages to provide complete solace from this loneliness is tremendously high. Many people become overly dependent on their partners, hoping their spouse will meet *all* their emotional needs. When a marriage is working well, it can certainly provide some refuge from isolation, but relying too heavily on each other can become emotionally taxing. If two people in a marriage are emotionally alienated from each other, loneliness becomes amplified. As Robin William's character Lance Clayton said in *World's Greatest Dad*, "I used to think the worst thing in life was to end up alone. It's not. The worst thing in life is ending up with people who make you feel alone."

5. Your children are squeezing out your relationship with your spouse.

No doubt, having a child changes you and your marriage permanently, so the transition into parenthood is often a stressful one. Having a child is a dangerous thing to do accidentally because the initial stress of becoming parents could reveal cracks in an already-compromised relationship and challenge even a strong one. For many couples, the addition of the first child causes marital satisfaction to plummet.

Marital dissatisfaction after the transition to parenthood is not usually about the child. Most parents love their children deeply and are genuinely happy to care for them, even if it is demanding. The marital discontent that often develops stems more from losing the intimate connection with your spouse, which is naturally taken for granted and easier to sustain when it is just the two of you. A good marital relationship buffers stress and is protective of emotional well-being. But for most couples, unless you have regular help, there is simply less time to spend together after becoming parents. Additionally, resentment about unfair division of responsibilities, differing beliefs about child rearing, and social pressure to be perfect parents also generate tremendous strain on a marriage.

Research shows that the primary child-care and household responsibilities still fall on women, who do considerably more housework and spend more hours multitasking than their husbands. This inequity in workload often leads to disputes in a relationship. It is very easy to become resentful if you are responsible for the house and kids, in addition to managing your career. You may feel as if your spouse is not being a good friend to you by failing to share the increased responsibilities that come with children. The ongoing stress of managing competing work and family demands can push even the most capable person to their limits.

Most relationships do eventually adjust to the routine of children, but whether they endure depends heavily on whether an intimate connection between parents can be sustained in the midst of all the stress. It is all too easy to have your relationship revolve around the "to do" list for the day and the needs of the kids, as the companionship and fun that existed before they arrived is slowly lost.

As a couple, you need time together to keep your relationship vibrant. Having a strong emotional bond is what gets you through hard times. If the marital relationship is never prioritized, it is at greater risk for deteriorating, and in the end, that is not good for you or your children. Children benefit tremendously when their parents have a healthy relationship. Seeing their parents happy with each other is an extremely stabilizing experience that gives them a solid foundation from which to flourish.

If you are open and realistic about it, parenting is an experience that is truly life-changing. The depth of love you can feel for a child can be absolutely breathtaking, and sharing that bond with your husband can bring you closer. Children have a way of helping us become aware of our place in the life cycle and can bring tremendous joy and meaning to life. However, balancing the needs of your kids with your own, as well as those of the marriage, requires tremendous maturity, planning, and commitment.

6. You genuinely believe anything is possible.

Have you ever heard any of the following messages?

- You can achieve anything if you set your mind to it.

- When the going gets tough, the tough get going.
- Pick yourself up, and keep going.
- Just push through it.
- The sky's the limit!

In a society where there is a pervasive belief that you can "have it all" if you work hard enough, discussing limits is not popular. So, most people just keep pushing themselves harder, hoping that with enough determination, a vibrant career, loving marriage, happy kids, beautiful home, supportive community, health, and happiness will all somehow fall into place. The fear of not being or having enough combined with a belief in being limitless keep many people trapped in stress.

Adding to the stress is the fact that we are also always measuring ourselves against one another. We look at the neighbors and assume they are achieving these goals with ease. From the discussions I regularly have in my office, I have come to believe that there is a huge chasm between what most people think they *should* be able to achieve and what they actually can. The reality is that many people are struggling. They are afraid of failing and don't realize that the goals they are pursuing are unrealistic in the first place. This social situation is a recipe for overwhelming stress.

I chuckled the other day when I read a poster that said, "Anyone who thinks anything is possible has obviously never tried to staple water to a tree!" There is no way around the reality that we are biological beings with real physical, emotional, cognitive, and spiritual limits. You can learn all the stress and time management strategies in the world, or exert superior willpower and self-control, and it will still never change the fact that there is only so much you can do.

Limits are nothing to be ashamed of; they are simply a reality of our existence. The problem is the dysfunctional message that there is something wrong with having limits. This lie can have dangerous consequences, as failure to respect our limits makes us more vulnerable in so many areas of our lives. The data shows that rates of stress-related illnesses, obesity, chemical addiction, divorce, and loneliness are high. In the face of constant social pressure to blindly keep working harder, it is easy to lose sight of what you love. Honoring your limits and working *with* them, rather than against them, puts you in the powerful position of making real choices in your life.

BOTTOM LINE

Stress can be toxic to a relationship.

Chronic activation of the body's hardwired stress response poses a threat to relationships. When a person is highly stressed, they do not function in ways that support the relationship. You must proactively manage outside pressures on your relationship in order to cultivate a healthful environment that makes it easier for love to grow. Respecting personal limits and making choices that allow you to function within those limits are vital to managing stress.

PART 2

THE ART AND SCIENCE OF THE STRONG, IRRESISTIBLE WOMAN

As we have seen, a constantly changing environment full of stress threatens marriages and can leave you feeling powerless in your relationship. To deal with that, it's important to discover what you absolutely can influence regarding what happens to you. Real change starts with you, so Part 2 will explore how simple, yet highly-effective, shifts in the way you show up in your relationship can make you a much stronger partner in your marriage.

4

CALM DOWN TO
INVITE CONNECTION.

There are times when
we stop, we sit still.
We listen and breezes
from a whole other world
begin to whisper.
~James Carroll

Stress is truly the enemy of connection. As noted earlier, high levels of stress put a person into a highly-reactive state, making it difficult to think objectively and respond reasonably. Stressed-out people are hard to engage and not very emotionally attractive. If you are typically a frantic or tense person, it may be difficult for other people to be around you. In fact, the agitated energy of someone who is constantly frazzled tends to generate anxiety in others.

Shifting from doing to being

The cultural obsession with goals, goals, and more goals constantly keeps everyone in "doing" mode. However, in order to have a more balanced life experience, we also need to complement this approach with simply "being." Yoga teachers often tell their students to not only notice each breath, but also the *pause* in between breaths. Even in our bodies, we have motion, but also rest; doing and also being.

During stressful times, it is essential to calm yourself down so that you are emotionally available for connection and can engage your spouse in a constructive way. You have to dial down the level of emotional reactivity to keep things positive in a relationship. Let's explore some of the most effective ways you can deepen your capacity to be calm.

1. Slam on the built-in brakes!

Fortunately, our bodies come equipped with both an accelerator pedal (stress response) that gets us out of danger and a brake pedal (relaxation response) that allows us to slow down. In order to calm the stress response, you must elicit the "relaxation response," originally described by famous Harvard cardiologist Herbert Benson in the early 1970s. This counterpart to the stress response decreases heart rate, blood pressure, respiration, adrenaline levels, and muscle tension. So, while the stress response helps us move quickly, the relaxation response helps us calm back down. The stress response is automatic, but the relaxation response can be elicited purposefully. The most powerful way to engage the relaxation response is simply by breathing deeply.

2. Take a deep breath.

Most of us never stop to think about our breathing. About 25,000 times a day, our lungs automatically inhale oxygen and exhale carbon dioxide. We take this process for granted and seldom notice how sensitive our respiration is to pressures, worry, and the general level of stress in our lives. Stress causes us to breathe in a shallow, rapid manner and decreases oxygen flow into the body. Have you ever noticed that you often hold your breath when you are very tense? Proper breathing plays an essential role in decreasing high levels of stress and restoring your body to a relaxed state.

Babies provide the perfect example of healthy breathing. When a baby is sleeping, you can clearly see its little belly filling up like a balloon, inflating and deflating in a slow, steady rhythm. Because babies have little stress in their lives, they tend to be physically relaxed and naturally engage in deep breathing. When we are sleeping or relaxed, adults also breathe in this manner.

In order to learn how to breathe deeply, it helps to understand how your respiratory system functions. Your lungs extend all the way down to the bottom of your ribs and are basically in a "cage," encased by your ribs at the top and the diaphragm at the bottom. When you breathe, muscles between your ribs (intercostals) move your rib cage up and out, while your diaphragm muscle pushes on your stomach to create plenty of room for your lungs to fill at the bottom. During a normal, relaxed breath, your stomach gently rises and your lungs fill completely, bringing in plenty of life-sustaining oxygen. When you exhale, your muscles relax and stress exits your body.

3. Make sure you are breathing.

Stop right now and pay attention to how you are breathing. First, just observe whether you are breathing or holding your breath. Next, place one hand on your chest and one hand on your belly. When you take a deep breath in, which hand moves first? If the hand on your chest rises first, you are upper-chest breathing and only partially filling your lungs. If the lower hand rises first, you are engaging in deep diaphragmatic breathing and filling your lungs completely. Deep breathing stimulates the vagus nerve, the "switch" in the brain that triggers stress reduction.

Your body knows how to breathe properly when it is relaxed. Physically relaxing, loosening your clothes, and keeping emotional stress managed help this process tremendously. You can utilize the power of deep breathing by catching yourself when you are shallow breathing and deliberately choosing to take deep breaths instead. The more you practice deep breathing, the easier it is to shift from shallow to deep breathing.

Practice, practice, practice! The wonderful thing about deep breathing is that once you learn it, you don't have to take extra time out of your busy schedule to use it. You can practice deep breathing when you are at a traffic light, feeling irritated with your husband, or trying to stay patient with the kids. You can also use it while you are getting yelled at by your boss, about to make a presentation, or feeling overwhelmed by some bad news. Habitual, slow, deep breathing prevents stress build-up, increases your energy level, and reduces both anxiety and insomnia. The good news is that there are no side effects to eliciting the relaxation response, except improved health and vitality!

4. Escape your chattering mind.

Just as physical calming is vital, so also is mental calming. Do you obsess about things? Do you chronically worry about the future or dwell in the past? When you experience high stress (e.g., an illness, a death, intense work pressure), your sense of well-being is often temporarily hijacked by uncontrollable thoughts that race to various times in the past or future. Tune into your mind's chatter when you are strung out, and there is a strong likelihood that you will find yourself everywhere but here. The possibilities of where your mind goes are endless: You may be regretting a decision you made or worrying about how you will make ends meet if you lose your job.

A chattering mind is simply a function of your brain being alive. In the same way that your heart pumps blood 24 hours a day, your brain processes every life experience. Your brain cannot stop doing this, and believe me, you wouldn't want it to because that's something we call brain death! Thoughts are pretty much like a radio playing in the background of your life. Sometimes you tune in and hear what is playing.

Other times, the music may fade into the background.

The biggest problem with being too attuned to brain chatter is that you end up lost in thought and actually miss what's happening in your life. As a result, your capacity to influence the present diminishes considerably because your mind is not focused here. It is crucial to remember that the only thing that is real in life is the present moment. You have no ability to change the past and cannot influence the future until it gets here! So, it is vital to learn how to calm your mind so you can be more present in your life.

5. Practice mindfulness.

In the face of stress, fully engaging the present moment is extremely calming. Life feels much more manageable when you are literally just dealing with what's right in front of your nose, rather than playing out "what if" scenarios in your imagination.

Try it right now. Slow down for just a minute and choose to focus on the present moment. Become fully mindful of what is happening in your body at this very instant. Notice your breath. Are you breathing deeply or in a shallow manner? Did you just sigh? Scan the rest of your body. Are you feeling tired or refreshed? Do you have any aches or pains anywhere? Does your body need anything?

Here's the hard part: When your mind starts to wander again (and it will!), don't struggle or get mad at yourself for not being able to stay glued in the present. Remember that mental wandering is just a natural function of your brain. So, just gently pull yourself back into the present, as often as necessary. Try this exercise for a couple of minutes to see if you need to practice this skill.

It sounds simple, but attempting to focus in the present can be like holding a wet bar of soap. You think you have it, and then it slips right out of your hands! However, the minute you truly become absorbed in the moment, the brain chatter fades into the background, just like your awareness of your surroundings diminishes when you are lost in a really good movie. So, in order to calm your mind, repeatedly catch your mind wandering and make an active decision to come back to *now*.

There are other simple ways to become more mindful. For instance, next time you are driving, notice the scenery around you, or listen closely to the song playing on the radio, or savor the warmth of the sunshine on your face. Let yourself be fully present and aware. The shower is a great place for mindfulness. When your mind begins to wander, relish the warm water soothing your body. And as you wash your hair, observe the sensation of your fingers massaging your scalp and focus on the smell of the shampoo. In any situation, you can take five to ten focused, deep breaths to jump out of your obsessive thoughts and into the present for a while.

Some activities, such as cooking, reading, gardening, having sex, exercising, or listening to music make it easy for you to practice being mindful. If while you do these things, you also practice being fully engaged in each small moment, you will gain a vital skill for bringing yourself peace of mind.

Mindfulness is actually not a new skill for you. Early in your life, being engaged with the present came naturally and easily. Children are masters at relishing the "now" because they are very sensory beings. Have you ever seen a little kid savor an ice cream cone? It's delightful to watch them lost in the moment, licking the cold, sweet ice cream without concern, even when it melts all over their hands or clothes. The experience seems to envelop their being. Use children as a mental reference point for what being fully present looks like...and perhaps practice with a dessert of your choice!

Let go of what you hoped for, and open yourself up to what is.

High hopes and expectations have a way of stirring up stress in a relationship. When your partner fails to do something you wanted, it is easy to stoke your anger until your emotions reach a boiling point. Rather than accepting that he did not get the laundry done as you hoped, you keep telling yourself, "I can't believe he didn't finish the laundry! I asked him to do one thing to help me, and he couldn't even do that. He's so selfish!" Judging his actions and being invested in a particular outcome leads your negative feelings to snowball. Resisting reality by continuing to focus on what you *wish* had happened actually causes the negativity to multiply.

Let's do a quick exercise to illustrate my point. For the next minute, TRY <u>NOT</u> TO NOTICE YOUR EYES BLINKING. Go ahead and do this for 30 seconds, and then continue reading. What did you notice? Were you more or less aware of your eyes blinking? Is it hard to get that blinking out of your mind now?

Usually, the more you resist something, the more intensely you end up focusing on it. In a relationship, as in life, when you fight the things you cannot change, the bigger the problem seems. The more you focus on the fact that he is messier than you, the more vital it seems to the continuation of your marriage that he learn how to get organized immediately! Seriously, during that moment when your mind is obsessed with the desire that he become a more organized person, the anger accompanying those thoughts causes you to lose sight of other, equally-important information. You forget that he is a positive, fun, caring person, and that his messiness is actually not that big a deal in the big picture. You fail to remember that he loves you very much and is probably very hurt by the unkind words you just uttered. You forget that at one point in your life, you adored him enough to marry him.

Taking an emotional step back, dropping the harsh judgment, and then letting go of control is the way out. Detaching from a particular outcome means that you notice your expectations, and then make an active decision to release any rigidity around them. You choose, instead, to respond to your partner with compassion. As hard as it is, if your priority is to keep your marriage strong, you must practice choosing flexibility and the relationship over self-righteous indignation.

BOTTOM LINE

The ability to calm yourself is essential to full engagement with your spouse.

Stress makes it tremendously difficult to connect with your partner in a constructive way. Mastering self-calming skills and having appropriate expectations of your spouse are essential to both personal and relationship health.

5

REMOVE THE BARRIERS
TO CHANGING YOUR
RELATIONSHIP

*The truth is that our finest moments
are most likely to occur when we are
feeling deeply uncomfortable,
unhappy, or unfulfilled.
For it is only in such moments,
propelled by our discomfort, that
we are likely to step out of our ruts
and start searching for
different ways or truer answers.
~M. Scott Peck*

It takes real strength to make deep changes in your life. The longer I work as a psychologist, the more I am convinced that human beings are inherently designed to resist major change. I often tell my clients that in the same way most people's bodies maintain their internal temperature at a precise 98.6 degrees Fahrenheit, their mental and emotional states aim to stay steady too. In relationship terms, what this means is that even when a marriage is clearly not working, what usually feels easiest is to do what you have always done. Many people only initiate significant change once life becomes unbearable. Suffering is a potent motivator, so feelings of distress often provide the initial impetus for change.

Whenever anyone contemplates change, a common initial reaction is resistance. Resistance can show up in many forms, but its function is always the same: to maintain the status quo. People don't always gravitate toward what is healthy as much as they tend to cling to what is familiar. This chapter describes seven common barriers to making necessary changes in a relationship.

Hiding from the truth

Many people cope with difficult situations by avoiding them. This can only work until the elephant in the room grows so big that it is impossible to ignore it. The larger a problem gets, the harder it is to address it. Poet Robert Frost once wrote the line: "The best way out is always through." No matter what the current reality of your marriage, I challenge you to step into the truth and work through your problems rather than run from them.

The scariest part of change is opening your eyes. See if you can find the courage to look at yourself honestly. Do you still know who you are? Is that spark you had years ago still there? Gaze deeply at your spouse. Why did you marry him? What were the qualities you fell in love with? Do you still feel a connection, or is there just a huge chasm there?

Certainly, it can be quite scary to feel lost or to believe that recovering the connection with your spouse is impossible. Yet, it is imperative you find the courage to be honest with yourself about where things really stand in your life. Until you do that, it is impossible to make any constructive move.

Harboring resentment

Even when it is obvious that your relationship is in trouble, resentment may prevent you from initiating change. You may feel resentful that you are the one reading this book, searching for ways to make your relationship better. You might think, "Why can't he do it? Why do *I* have to do everything? Why should I care more than him?" Yes, both of you are responsible for the relationship and keeping it healthy. However, ask yourself, "Why *not* you?" You have power. You have brains. You have hopes and dreams. Why wouldn't you want to do whatever *you* need to increase the odds of having the life *you* desire?

A great deal of emotional pain and loneliness accompanies resentment. Struggling with relationship problems can leave anyone feeling demoralized and resentful. You might actually be the one more invested in the relationship. However, if you are engaging in quid pro quo thinking—keeping track of everything he does and everything you do—the problem will never improve. For change to happen, at some point, you have to be the bigger person, putting resentment aside to allow the relationship a chance to be revived. Shifting the focus away from your anger and back on yourself can get you in touch with the tremendous power you have to improve your life.

What if you feel so resentful that you genuinely cannot take any constructive steps toward your partner right now? If you know you want to stay in the marriage, but don't feel very loving yet, it doesn't necessarily mean that your relationship is doomed. Simply take note of your resentment and shift your attention toward yourself, where it belongs anyway. If you can at least stop adding to the negativity, consider that a success for now. If the resentment is so strong that you feel paralyzed by it, seek professional support to help you get unstuck.

Relinquishing your personal power

Many women surrender their personal power when they get into a relationship, placing themselves into a passive role. Before you met your husband, you were probably an independent person who was content, even without him in your life. Women are routinely convinced that one day a man will sweep them off their feet and then completely dedicate himself to keeping them happy forever. As a result of this belief, a woman's happiness becomes contingent on how well her partner does this job. Ironically, men often have no idea their wives have such expectations, so end up disappointing them repeatedly, without even intending to do so!

It is unfair and unrealistic to make another person responsible for your emotional well-being. Your husband is in your life to add to it, not to complete it, so it's important to shift the focus off him and put yourself back in the driver's seat of your life. As hard as it is to swallow, at the end of the day, this is your life, and *you* are ultimately responsible for making it what you want.

The only person you can control is you. Period. You cannot force your husband to change, so don't worry about him for now, and see what happens. A marriage is like a dance. While you can never control the steps your partner takes, you have tremendous power by being more deliberate about your own steps. I have worked with numerous women who felt their marriages were over. They came to see me because they wanted to work on themselves. In many cases, as soon as they began to feel stronger and more alive, their marriages unexpectedly began to make a positive shift too.

Your relationship may have changed radically, and you may feel unsure about it. However, when it comes to your marriage, you really cannot sit on the fence. You're either helping your relationship or hurting it. You have a choice to make. You can either dig in your heels or wait for him to "wake up," or you can reclaim your power and initiate positive changes. It's up to you. Either way, time does not stop; life literally goes on. Each day that goes by is one that you will never get back.

So, see if you can find the courage to open up your heart and mind to the possibility that your life can improve. As you shift the focus to yourself and increase your positive contribution to the relationship, the negativity in your relationship is likely to subside, allowing the two of you to start bridging differences. If for any reason, things don't work out with your partner, you will be glad you did your best to give the relationship a fair chance. Don't give up, especially on yourself.

Being unaware of thinking errors that skew how you see your husband

Although it is entirely possible you are in a relationship with someone who is truly ill-equipped for marriage, I want you to consider whether common blind spots in your thinking style could possibly be contributing to some of your relationship challenges. There are three widespread biases in everyone's thoughts that make it difficult to interpret your partner's actions accurately.

First, people usually assume that *they* are the ones behaving normally in any situation. There is a strong inclination to assume that others are usually in control of their actions, but that your own behavior is more affected by external circumstances. This is technically known as the fundamental attribution bias. So if your husband forgot to call you, you're more likely to assume it's because he's irresponsible than if you did the same thing. In your own case, you might say it's because you were very busy and lost track of time.

Secondly, we tend to seek information that supports our preconceived ideas (confirmation bias). Once you start to think your spouse is a loser, without realizing it, you look for evidence to support that belief. On the other hand, if you think he's amazing, you find a way to confirm that too! Understanding this thinking bias may help you see how believing "My husband doesn't care about me, only himself" can quickly snowball into intense feelings of resentment. What you focus on grows, so assuming the best about your spouse makes this bias work in your favor.

People also tend to believe that others can easily read their thoughts and feelings just by looking at them (illusion of transparency). So, when you are mad at your husband, you may think, "I don't need to tell him what I'm thinking. It's pretty obvious," thereby closing off further communication. You always know what you are thinking and feeling, so you assume he always does too. You may be surprised or upset when your partner misreads you. In reality, a person's subjective experience is not that transparent.

It's easy to forget that everyone else is just as lost in their own thoughts and feelings as you are in yours. Over time, the bias toward believing that your internal state is transparent can convince you that your husband's failure to respond to your "clear" signals means he simply does not care. Communicating your thoughts and feelings directly is vital to preventing such misunderstanding. When something is important, don't assume you are easy to read, and make sure you state it obviously.

Maintaining an antagonistic stance in the relationship

All too frequently, women and men bring traits, such as dominance and competitiveness, which are highly useful at work, into their marriages. Those in leadership roles in their jobs may have a "boss" attitude in their marriage, delegating tasks and expecting compliance from their spouse. Many couples vie for control of the relationship, forgetting that you don't find your way into someone's heart by battling with them! After having used a sledgehammer, they wonder why the other person has withdrawn or responded aggressively. Relating in a hardnosed manner in your marriage compromises emotional safety, making it much harder to work cooperatively to make necessary changes to the relationship.

Giving up the behaviors that generate antagonism is vital. Moving into a cooperative, receptive, gentle stance is much more effective for deepening connection and trust in a marriage. Although being accommodating and compassionate have historically been associated with femininity, remember that traditional feminine qualities are not tied to a person's sex. In fact, these ways of relating are fairly common among men and women in cultural groups that value harmony over conflict (e.g., Thailand). Femininity is a powerful tool available to *both* men and women who seek to improve the connection with their spouse.

Mistaking vulnerability for weakness

People become stronger and wiser as they open themselves up to what life has to teach, especially when it is hard. Do you look down on yourself for having problems in your marriage? Do you consider yourself weak because your life is not going as you planned? Do you believe that feelings of vulnerability, fear, or helplessness signal that you are not strong enough?

One of the things I frequently hear when people first start therapy is that they feel "weak" or like a "failure" because they couldn't figure things out on their own. Nothing could be further from the truth! Seeking help is what smart, strong people do. It takes tremendous courage to acknowledge vulnerability or limitations.

We live in a society that equates strength with fierce independence, physical prowess, and being unstoppable. Yet, some of the hardest things we cope with in life call for different qualities. When your relationship is struggling, you are trapped in your life, and you fear you cannot find your way out, ferociously plowing forward is simply the wrong strategy.

Some experiences in life cannot be overcome so easily. Instead, they require acceptance, humility, and the courage to embrace hardship. The only way through some moments in life is to literally surrender to them, allowing them to shape your character and reveal to you the most precious lessons about life. Emotional healing, especially, requires patience, gentleness, and a humble stance because you are literally "growing" new wisdom. For the average person, this process generates anxiety and takes real strength to endure, but can also enhance the capacity for deep compassion and kindness.

Failing to seize the moment

It can be tempting to put off making changes in your marriage, assuming it will always be there, even if it is not perfect. Let me remind you that each day a relationship is left to struggle increases the odds of things worsening. Don't wait until you are faced with the crisis of a divorce to do something. Take advantage of today. It is important to be honest about any internal roadblocks you face and take active steps to move past them. Use the information in this book to help you open up your mind and heart. Knowledge is power and can be tremendously helpful in easing fear so that you can start the process of change.

BOTTOM LINE

True change begins the moment you embrace truth.

The kind of love most people long for takes tremendous courage and personal responsibility to attain. Dare to open yourself up to the change process by removing your personal barriers to change so you can move your relationship in a more positive direction.

6

KNOW WHO YOU ARE AND WHAT YOU NEED.

*A woman with a voice is
by definition a strong woman.
But the search to find that voice can
be remarkably difficult.
~Melinda Gates*

Most people want a marriage that is passionate, intimate, and endures the test of time. However, the ability to cultivate such a relationship relies heavily on each person having a strong sense of self, emotional maturity, and skills to navigate the natural ups and downs of life together. Love is only as strong as the two people in it.

When you think of the ideal partner, which one appeals to you more? The person who is chronically stressed and angry, or the one with whom you can relax and have some fun? The one who tells you what they really think, or who gives you the answer they think you want? The person who is engaged with their own life, or the one who clings and is constantly focused on you? Now, think of yourself and be honest. Which kind of partner are you?

Practice intimate separateness.

Dr. David Schnarch, author of *Passionate Marriage: Keeping Love and Intimacy Alive in Committed Relationships*, believes strongly that defining your identity separately from your partner is what keeps a marriage healthy and draws a couple closer. Continuing to grow as two separate, yet intimately-connected, individuals ultimately allows a relationship to last.

The process of distinguishing yourself from your partner is called differentiation and can only be achieved when you fully accept that he is a separate human being who can never provide all you need. Having a differentiated self means:

• Knowing who you are and what you stand for—your strengths, weaknesses, likes, dislikes, needs, unique qualities, values, goals, aspirations, etc.

- Respecting, valuing, and feeling comfortable with yourself.
- Having the capacity to truly stand on your own, not relying on your partner to constantly reassure, validate, or accept everything you do or say.
- Being able to handle emotional distance, disagreement, or honest feedback, without freaking out or taking it too personally.
- Being able to take an honest look at yourself and taking responsibility for making necessary changes.

Learn to be flexible.

In a relationship, it is important to have some capacity for flexibility. There are times when you and your partner need to lean on each other, like when you are ill. Other times, you are distant from each other because you are simply busy or need space. The level of closeness can also fall somewhere between the two.

When each person in a relationship has a strong sense of self, you can move into different stances based on your needs. Movement away is not viewed as a threat, and movement toward is not considered suffocating because each person is emotionally-secure, generally self-reliant, and trusting.

The two most problematic stances in a relationship are Excessively Close and Emotionally Distant. If you have a weaker sense of self, you are probably driven by fear, which makes you prone to being too close or too distant. It is difficult for you to accept the fluid nature of a relationship, so you may not allow your relationship the breathing room and intimacy necessary to grow in a healthy manner. These two stances may manifest in the following ways:

Excessively Close (Needy/Clingy)
- Needing constant reassurance
- Feeling intense jealousy
- Being intrusive
- Making your partner the center of your universe
- Nurturing your spouse excessively by relating more like a mom than a partner
- Acting like a victim, doormat, or helpless person
- Refusing to do anything independently of your partner
- Not knowing what you need or want
- Ignoring all other relationships

<u>Emotionally Distant (Emotional Strangers)</u>

- Hiding your true thoughts and feelings from your partner
- Being so independent your partner feels unnecessary in your life
- Avoiding deep connection
- Ignoring your partner's needs
- Showing little interest in the details of your partner's life
- Spending all your time with other people or activities, including work
- Avoiding relationship problems that need to be addressed

If you are regularly relating to your partner in any of these ways, it is important to ask yourself what unfulfilled needs or wishes are driving you.

Women are often taught to make men the center of their world, but men usually find this too intense and withdraw. What works better is having a life of your own that you gladly share with each other. A strong sense of self gives you the flexibility essential to a healthy relationship.

Understand the danger of being too nice.

Women face tremendous social pressure to be generous and accommodating because they are supposed to be "nice." They regularly sacrifice their own needs in order to take care of others first. This habitual surrender of basic needs places women at risk for losing themselves in relationships, especially after they become mothers, because the pull to sacrifice becomes even more compelling.

Although focusing on others is admirable, done to excess, it can cause a deadness to creep into your life, making it difficult to remember who you really are, what you need, and what stirs your passion in life. *The more disconnected you become from your core sense of self, the more lifeless you feel, and the less of you there is for your partner to fully engage.* Then one day you find the only thing that remains is a shell of a person and a vast distance between you and your partner.

Distinguish selfishness from self-care.

Fear that others will see them as selfish is one reason women resist focusing on their own needs. It is important to distinguish "selfishness" from "self-care." By definition, a person who is selfish lacks consideration for others and cares *only* about their own needs. Self-*care* is about respecting yourself enough to look after your basic needs, recognizing that your capacity to give to others is highly limited when you don't. Ironically, the women most likely to worry about being selfish are the ones least likely to actually be selfish! How often do you think a truly selfish person sits around worrying about how others will be affected by their actions?

Anyone who has flown is familiar with the safety instructions at the beginning of a flight, telling you to put your *own* oxygen mask on before helping others. The same is true in life. If you want to be able to give of yourself to other people, taking very good care of yourself is critical.

Every person has their own definition of self-care. If you are a busy lawyer, self-care may mean taking a lunch break each day. If you are a mom with a newborn, self-care could be napping when your baby is sleeping. If you are juggling many different roles, self-care may well mean hiring a housekeeper to relieve some practical burdens.

More so than women, men feel comfortable honoring their basic needs without apology. For example, if, while you are cooking dinner, your husband is hungry, he may grab a snack without thinking that it might irritate you. Or, if he is tired, he may just fall asleep, free of worry about whether he "should." From his perspective, he has a need, so why shouldn't he take care of it?

There may be something to be learned from this stance.

Break the shackles of guilt.

Guilt is another barrier to self-care. Women often become mired in guilt when they prioritize their own needs, even though this is an essential part of staying healthy and vibrant. Understandably, it is difficult to make a positive change when "it doesn't feel right." Although guilt is often thought of as a moral compass telling you right from wrong, *constant* guilt is different. The psychological function of persistent guilt is often to prevent change, to literally keep you frozen in your tracks! This type of guilt is common among women socialized to sacrifice themselves. Women and men brought up in group-oriented cultures, like China, or religious institutions, such as the Catholic Church, are also prone to tremendous guilt because of the very strong mandate to think of others before themselves.

Because any personal change requires some individual focus, guilt automatically emerges. Most women have difficulty tolerating the emotional distress guilt brings, so they opt for short-term emotional relief and continue ignoring their own needs for years on end. It is a challenge to break out of this pattern, but remembering that chronic guilt is resistance, not a commentary on your character, helps. If you can push yourself to start prioritizing your own needs, you will eventually move beyond the guilt, and discover the tremendous power of having your needs consistently met!

Hold onto yourself to hold onto the marriage.

Men tend to approach marriage with fewer expectations and demands of women than women often realize. You may be surprised to learn that your husband may actually not find all your "giving" very helpful, as his primary needs center on wanting a positive connection with you. If you are vibrant, fully engaged, relaxed, and appreciative of his efforts, he will feel affirmed and content in the relationship. Your mere presence adds meaning to his life, and he becomes highly motivated to take care of you as well.

Learning to take care of yourself is vital to the health of your marriage. As you consistently meet your basic needs, you will have increased energy to infuse into the relationship. By pursuing your hopes and dreams, you make it easier for the two of you to chase your shared goals together. If you do not value yourself enough to keep yourself in the picture, there are tremendous limits to how much love you can truly give or receive. Holding onto your marriage and holding onto yourself go hand in hand.

BOTTOM LINE

A strong sense of self is essential to a healthy marriage.

A man is not there to "complete" you. Unless you have a strong, separate sense of self, it is virtually impossible to sustain a healthy love that remains steady over time.

7

LET HIM SEE YOU.

There is nothing more rare, nor more
beautiful, than a woman being
unapologetically herself; comfortable
in her perfect imperfection.
~Steve Maraboli

Very young children exude authenticity. They speak their minds, express their emotions generously, and radiate positive energy. They are comfortable in their own skin and delight in their uniqueness and that of others. We can't help but be drawn to these wonderful qualities.

Over time, life has a way of chipping away at our authenticity. The world continually bombards us with messages about how we must behave in order to be accepted. Our parents teach us how to be a "good" boy or girl. The media tells us how to dress, what to eat, and how to be "cool." What's "in fashion" changes constantly, so it's hard work to keep up.

This sea of influence makes it all too easy to lose touch with yourself. Do you still know exactly what you like and don't like? Do you voice your opinions openly? Do you dress in ways that feel right to you? Or, are you so out of touch with yourself that you automatically transform yourself to gain acceptance?

There certainly is no shame in wanting to fit in, as belonging is a hardwired need for human beings. People can literally go crazy if they are completely isolated for extended periods. For anyone who has been hurt by another person, acceptance may be exactly what is needed to start healing. However, the danger is that when you regularly hide yourself in order to gain approval, you start to live a lie. The fear of rejection can imprison your true self.

Facades take a tremendous amount of energy to maintain. Putting a false self out there day after day is draining and can lead to deep sadness, a sense of emptiness, and a feeling of being alone. Living a phony existence also supports a cookie-cutter culture in which people feel uncomfortable expressing their real selves. In a relationship, an inauthentic stance is absolutely detrimental to deeper emotional intimacy. If you have not done so already, it is important consider allowing your partner to get to know the real you.

Figure out if you are holding back too often.

No doubt about it, people need connection and suffer tremendously when rejected. This need for acceptance can make it difficult to take emotional risks. Ask yourself the following questions to explore how comfortable you are revealing the real you:

- How much do I care about what other people think about me?
- Does fear of judgment or rejection cause me to routinely hold back in my life?
- Who am I when no one else is around?
- Who am I typically when others are present?
- When do I feel most comfortable showing up as myself?
- When do I have a tendency to run and hide? Why?
- What price do I pay when I'm not authentic?
- How would my marriage change if my husband saw the real me?
- What would others learn about me if I let them see who I really am?

- If I were authentic all the time, how would my life change?

Know the difference between emotionally guarded and private.

For some of you, certain life experiences have led you to build very high walls around your authentic self to keep you safe. You may be cautious about letting anyone in too closely and may tell others that you are a just a very private person. That may indeed be true, but in order to distinguish whether you are emotionally guarded or private, it is important to identify what drives your need to conceal your true self.

When a person is private, they have the capacity to unapologetically reveal who they are, but only choose to do so with people they deem safe. An emotionally-guarded person, on the other hand, may not trust anyone and is driven to keep others out due to fear, shame, or embarrassment. The problem with emotional walls is that, although they help you momentarily feel safe, when they are too high, they also keep out the things you really want, like love and friendship.

If you have been mistreated, hurt, or shamed by anyone, it may take some real work for you to be able to show up as yourself within your marriage. Take responsibility for your emotional wounds and work on healing them if you wish to fully engage your partner. Counseling is certainly one safe place to do this kind of work. Remember that at the end of the day, everyone wants to feel loved, nobody wants to be rejected, and being emotionally walled off can leave you incredibly lonely.

Unleash the real you.

Being fully present in a relationship means censoring yourself less so that your partner can really get to know you. I have been surprised by the number of marriages in which both people are essentially emotional strangers, making it impossible to achieve deeper intimacy. *Simple fear* is the biggest culprit for perpetuating emotional distance, even in committed relationships.

Dr. Brene Brown, author of *The Gifts of Imperfection*, says that many people have been taught that imperfection and vulnerability are weaknesses, although these qualities are merely part of our shared humanity and connect us to one another. Allowing yourself to be seen exactly as you are, not as you think you are *supposed* to be, is incredibly liberating. Undoubtedly, revealing your authentic self also takes courage and should only be done around those who respect you and feel honored that you are willing to trust them by being so transparent. If you have an emotionally-safe relationship with your husband, your marriage may be the ideal place to begin taking the risk to strengthen your skills at being more authentic. Try these tips for revealing the real you within your marriage:

- Risk telling your partner what you really think next time you are asked your opinion.
- When you and your husband are trying to make a decision, let your true choice be heard.
- Express your real thoughts and feelings when he invites you to do so.
- Think of one thing you've never told anyone else and share it with your husband.
- Make a list of your core values and work toward making your life reflect them.
- Do more of the things that bring energy into your life.
- Take some quiet time to meditate or reflect, so you can be more in touch with your inner voice.
- Develop a talent you have secretly wished you had.
- The next time your husband asks you how you are doing, tell him the uncensored truth.

- Honor and accept your husband's differences. He has a need to be himself, just like you.

Authenticity is a magnet that can pull you closer to your spouse. A positive climate for authenticity is created when you have the courage to expose your own vulnerability without expecting your partner to reciprocate. Yes, I did say, *without expecting him to reciprocate!* You simply cannot force a person to be open, but sometimes they are inspired by your actions. The challenge on your end is to relate in a sincere, inviting manner because that is the healthiest thing for you and the relationship, not because you have a hidden agenda to smoke him out.

Not everyone will be comfortable with the "real" you. You may lose some relationships in the process, but most likely these will be the ones that are the most draining anyway. The interesting thing is that the more authentic you are willing to be, the more you will draw other authentic people to your life. Being part of a community of people who are willing to be honest and open with one another frees *everyone* up to focus on what is truly important in their lives.

The indisputable formula for becoming simply irresistible

Although authenticity is one of the most alluring qualities a person can possess, American society tell us that attractiveness primarily comes from being physically beautiful and sexually desirable, and that if these qualities become compromised in any way, your relationship is at huge risk for falling apart. Look around, and you will notice that helping a woman keep a man interested in her body is big business. How much money do you think is made from the sales of cosmetics, fragrance, lingerie, fashion items, anti-aging, and weight-loss products? The media reinforces the idea that if you are physically striking, a man will be unable to resist you. He will be drawn to you like a magnet and rendered helpless by the power of your beauty.

It is fine to take pride in your appearance. There is absolutely nothing wrong with taking care of your body and looking your best. These things are healthy. However, the lie is that weighing a certain amount, being physically stunning, or behaving like a sex goddess are the keys to keeping a man connected to you over the years.

It is your *emotional* attractiveness that helps you form a strong connection. A man may certainly be initially captivated by your appearance, but will ultimately stay because of how he feels when he is with you. If you value yourself, relate authentically, and make it easy for him to be himself with you, he will find that highly appealing. People are drawn to someone who projects quiet confidence, has a sense of self-worth, and is emotionally inviting,

If you do not like what you see in the mirror, that attitude will be projected outward, making it difficult for others to be around you. Doctoring your appearance is not enough to cover up any inner sense of unattractiveness. I read a poster the other day that made this point clearly: *Maybe you should eat makeup so you can be pretty on the inside too.* No amount of pretending will hide negative emotional energy inside you. Neediness, desperation, and tension are not attractive to anyone. Chronic irritability, jealousy, and manipulation are huge turn-offs. Would you seek these qualities if you were a man? Who you are on the inside does matter after all. It actually counts more than you may have realized until now.

You cannot make a man love you. If you want to entice him to move closer to you, you must have self-respect and behave in ways that allow him to feel positive around you. A little backbone and confidence mixed with kindness and sensitivity are alluring. If you genuinely accept his differences, respect him, and appreciate how he contributes to your life, he will be drawn to you.

It is necessary to work on yourself so you can release the fear that he will disappear. Let go of your need for him to live up to all your expectations. Clinging, worry, and control are all signs you are still in fear. As long as you stay entrenched in fear, you are moving in a direction away from him. Now this does not mean that you should try to act tough. Your vulnerability is not the problem. It is the way you respond to feeling vulnerable that is the issue. So, be honest about your feelings, but don't try to cage him or grab his legs as he is walking out the door!

The vital point I want you to understand is this:

Emotional attractiveness emerges from valuing yourself enough to unleash your whole radiant, beautiful, competent, powerful, vulnerable, real self in the relationship. Relaxed authenticity, combined with loving action, fuel emotional attractiveness, making you absolutely irresistible to your partner.

Got it?

SELF-WORTH + RELAXED AUTHENTICITY + LOVING ACTIONS = ATTRACTIVENESS AND IRRESISTIBILITY

Sound easy enough? Of course, implementing all this is where the true challenge lies!

The end result of engaging your authenticity and being loving is indisputable. Trust me. What healthy man wouldn't love to be with a woman who genuinely values and accepts herself, feels at home in her body, and radiates inner beauty? Who wouldn't want to be with a woman who has the courage to be vulncrable, does not play emotional games, and loves him generously, despite his flaws and imperfections? Most of us want someone with whom we can simply be ourselves, without fear of negative consequences. The more you are able to surrender to who you really are, the easier it will be for your spouse to also do the same.

Let yourself need a man.

Successful, professional women often approach a relationship with a sense of pride that they don't need a man. Like most men, they value independence and want to be perceived as "strong," so they, too, hide their vulnerability. But what does it mean to be strong? Does it mean you shouldn't need anyone? Does it mean you must always have it together, no matter what the circumstance? Is it easier to form an emotional bond with someone who reveals their vulnerability or someone who doesn't?

Ironically, excessive focus on being strong and independent actually hinders emotional intimacy. We all need others; it's simply how we are made. Yet, it can feel scary to admit this need in a society that idealizes independence and defines strength as being emotionally unaffected. I think people sometimes confuse "needing" with "neediness." Needing others is healthy and necessary. Chronic neediness, on the other hand, is a state of being overly-dependent on someone else and can feel suffocating and annoying.

When you allow yourself to need your partner, you may feel vulnerable, especially if you see this as being weak. After all, there is always some risk he could hurt or disappoint you. You have to be incredibly strong to tolerate the anxiety that often comes with putting yourself in such a position, but if you can do so, you have a chance to develop a deeper bond. Daring to let down your guard to allow your partner to see the real you sends the clear message that you value and trust him enough to take such an emotional risk. Most healthy men respond with compassion, tenderness, and protectiveness in these powerful, genuine moments and will usually feel even greater affection toward you.

BOTTOM LINE

Your authentic self is irresistible.

From the moment you were born, the world began to define who you are, how you should live, and what you must do to be accepted. With all this external influence, it is easy to lose touch with your authentic self. No one can love you if you are not even present. Showing up as yourself in the relationship and engaging in loving action makes you irresistible.

PART 3

ACTIONS THAT ARE THE KISS OF DEATH FOR A MARRIAGE

Before we get into how you build an awesome marriage, in Part 3, we will take a closer look at something just as important—what will typically blow a relationship apart! A marriage can often be improved simply by refraining from engaging in hurtful actions.

8

DON'T HIT BELOW THE BELT AND OTHER GROUND RULES FOR MANAGING CONFLICT.

Nothing is so strong as gentleness.
Nothing is so gentle as real strength.
~Ralph W. Sockman

Studies conducted by world-renowned marriage researcher Dr. John Gottman are absolutely clear: Managing conflict well in a relationship is the most important determinant of whether the relationship survives. Conflict is inevitable in any relationship because you and your spouse are different people. However, when it is handled well, conflict also presents a tremendous opportunity to strengthen the connection between you. Mismanaged conflict, on the other hand, can be quite hazardous to the health of your marriage.

Because many people fear a disagreement will escalate into something unmanageable, when a problem arises, they simply avoid it, hoping it will "take care of itself." Years of sweeping things under the rug undermines the health of your relationship. Each conflict the two of you face successfully increases the likelihood your marriage will survive the normal up and downs of life. Responding to disagreements constructively ensures your relationship will be strengthened, not damaged. Rather than running, open yourself up to learning some effective ways to move through conflict.

You can't fix everything, so be realistic about which problems you can solve.

Dr. Gottman's research shows that 70% of the problems in most marriages are chronic, unsolvable, and simply stem from the fact that you are two different people. So, no matter which partner you choose, most problems that arise will be difficult to resolve and just have to be accepted.

If the unsolvable problems are in areas that are important to one of you, but neither one of you is willing to compromise, they are more likely to drive a wedge between you. For example, if you think financial planning is important, but your spouse does not, and he sabotages your efforts, this could certainly cause trouble. Ideally, in your relationship, the unsolvable issues are ones you can live with. Knowing your spouse intimately, as will be discussed in more detail in Chapter 11, avoids unnecessary misunderstandings and helps you realistically assess which problems are worth your energy.

Know the warning signs that predict divorce with amazing accuracy.

Many people believe that anger is the root cause of unhappy relationships, but Dr. Gottman has found that the problem lies in *how* conflict is handled. Venting complaints constructively can actually do wonders to clear the air and keep your relationship healthy. Conflict only becomes a problem when it is characterized by the presence of what Gottman calls the "Four Horsemen of the Apocalypse." Let's review each of the Four Horsemen briefly:

1. **Criticism** involves blaming and attacking your partner's personality or character, rather than discussing the specific behavior

that bothers you. It is healthy to voice complaints, but you need to stay focused on the behavior, rather than attacking the person. Which of the following two statements would *you* respond to more easily? "I'm upset that you didn't take out the trash," OR, "I can't believe you didn't take out the trash. You're just so irresponsible and lazy." Calling the person "irresponsible and lazy" clearly crosses the line from complaint to criticism.

In general, women are more likely to pull this Horseman into conflict. They often perceive men as not wanting to give them what they need when, in fact, a man may have no idea what his partner needs because she has never clearly articulated it to him. Many men respond to harsh criticism by shutting down and distancing, as they feel unloved, belittled, and discouraged.

2. **Defensiveness** often shows up in response to criticism. Most people get defensive when attacked. Denying responsibility, making excuses, and counterattacking with a criticism of your own are all examples of defensiveness. Adopting a defensive stance in the middle of conflict may be a natural

response, but this Horseman harms the relationship.

3. **Contempt**, according to Gottman's research, is the worst of the Four Horsemen and the best predictor of divorce. Examples of contempt include: unapologetically insulting your spouse in front of others, rolling your eyes or sneering, or cutting down your spouse with so-called "humor." The attitude is one of opcn disrespect and superiority.

4. **Stonewalling** occurs when a person shuts down because they are experiencing an intense physical reaction to conflict. They may appear as if they don't care, but in fact, the internal dialogue of a Stonewaller is typically something like, "Just shut up. Don't say anything else or it will make things worse." Stonewallers are desperate to stop the conflict from escalating, but may actually add to it by appearing as if they don't care. About 85% of Stonewallers are men, and research shows that stonewalling usually begins when the person's heart rate reaches 100 beats per minute or more! So, despite the "stone" exterior, internally there is a great deal of psychological and physical turmoil.

Gottman's research reveals that when these four factors are chronically present in a relationship, the likelihood of divorce increases dramatically. When attempts to repair the damage done by these Horsemen are met with repeated rejection, the odds that a couple will divorce increase further.

All couples engage in these types of behaviors occasionally in their relationship, but when the Four Horsemen take permanent residence, the relationship has a high likelihood of failing. Remember that everything you do in a relationship either helps or hurts it... *everything*. There is no neutral action. How you relate to your partner when conflict arises is especially vital to the well-being of the connection between you.

Turn toward him when you feel like bailing.

In her book, *Hold Me Tight: Seven Conversations for a Lifetime of Love*, psychologist Dr. Sue Johnson discusses three patterns of communication she calls "Demon Dialogues," which tend to show up during conflict and cause a relationship to deteriorate.

1. **Find the Bad Guy**. This communication style is characterized by an "attack-attack"

pattern. Both parties accuse and blame each other for the problem at hand. ("We're poor because you're so irresponsible with money!")

2. **Protest Polka**. This is the most common pattern in relationships and often follows "Find the Bad Guy." One partner (usually the woman) pursues her spouse, criticizing him and demanding connection. The other party (usually the man) responds defensively, quickly withdrawing from the interaction. She then pursues him even more and he distances further, until she withdraws and gives up at some point.

3. **Freeze and Flee**. This is a "withdraw-withdraw" pattern that emerges after the couple has been engaging in the "Protest Polka" for some time. Rather than address the issues at hand, both parties withdraw into uncomfortable silence, bitter resentment, and emotional distance. The relationship is marked by a state of resignation and emotional pain.

To stop these types of interactions, it is important to look beyond the content of what is actually being said, to the underlying emotional dance between you. Each of these patterns is a failed attempt to engage your partner, a call for connection that was ineffectively answered. The tendency is to engage in a "tug-of-war" that unfortunately increases emotional distance. In successful relationships, partners learn to move toward each other in times of distress, essentially doing the opposite of what feels natural at the moment of conflict. When you choose to emotionally connect with your partner and commit yourself to listening closely, it is much easier to address the actual source of distress and move beyond it.

Follow these critical ground rules in the midst of conflict.

It is very difficult for two people to constructively resolve issues when they are both still fuming. The typical human reaction when someone gets mad at you is to be defensive. Unfortunately, that feeds the negative spiral and the argument escalates. Sometimes the only helpful thing you can do is delay resolving the problem until both of you have calmed down and can think more clearly.

Even in the midst of heated conflict, it is vital you maintain respect, as failing to do so can result in irreparable harm to your relationship. Let's take a look at five ground rules you can follow during conflict to decrease the likelihood of saying or doing hurtful things you cannot take back later:

1. **Be aware of timing**. Don't discuss issues when you are tired, irritated, or unable to control yourself. Don't argue while you're lying in bed. Don't hunt down your spouse if he is annoyed and seeking emotional space to calm down. Let things settle down. Just like you can't see what is inside a snow globe when it has just been shaken, you cannot really see another person's perspective when you are aggravated.

2. **If you can, hold hands and make eye contact as you converse**. By being physically in touch with your spouse, you are much less likely to engage in a free-for-all.

3. **Don't threaten your partner physically or emotionally.** Don't yell, call names or use foul language. Don't say you're going to leave unless you mean it. Do not leave the house without telling your partner that you will be back.

4. **Don't hit below the belt**. You know your spouse well and need to be aware of the power you have to hurt him. The words you choose can be a weapon that wounds your

partner deeply, so choose what you say carefully and *always* be respectful.

5. **Take your time, but be willing to eventually face the music**. Take time to calm down, and then address what happened. If you need it, ask for a reasonable amount of time to collect your thoughts prior to working through the problem.

Know how to successfully move through the conflict

Once you are finally ready, talk about hurt feelings and engage in a psychological autopsy of what happened. Do not start a discussion unless both of you are calm enough to be non-defensive. If you cannot approach the conversation with a willingness to look at your own part in what happened (no matter how small), it will be harder to be constructive.

When discussing conflict, it is important to understand something called the Zeigarnik Effect. This refers to the universal tendency of human beings to remember incomplete or interrupted experiences more than those that are finished. Unfinished business is like a pebble in your shoe, always nagging at you until you take care of it. You don't want the negativity to linger in your relationship and become a center of mental focus. Here are some suggestions for working things out with your spouse when the two of you are willing to engage in constructive dialogue. It may be helpful to share these strategies with your spouse because they will be even more effective when both of you are using them:

- **Start out gently**. Whether you get past the first few words without the conversation turning into another argument will depend largely on how the communication gets started. Be gentle. I probably don't need to tell you this, but approaching your partner by saying, "I want to talk about why you've been such a jerk lately," probably will not work! Start out softly. Instead try: "Honey, is now a good time for you to talk about the argument we had earlier? I think I'm calm enough to discuss it now."

- **Be open about your experience**. Let your husband know how you felt and articulate your perspective *without blaming*. Then ask him to briefly summarize what he heard you say so you can make sure he understood you accurately. Please don't view the purpose of this conversation as being to convince your partner that you were right, and he was wrong. Your goal in disclosing your experience is to identify what went wrong so you can determine what needs to be done differently in the future.

- **Listen, listen, listen**. Your husband gets a turn too. Let him tell you his side of things. It is natural to want to interrupt your partner to correct his view, but that is not listening. His truth is his truth, and you will only anger him if you are not really working to comprehend his perspective. Your job is to put yourself in his shoes to see if you can understand what happened. You may or may not agree with what he says, but that's beside the point when you are listening. Show him you are listening by briefly summarizing what you heard him say. If you understand his perspective, validate that by saying, "Now that I'm looking at things from your side, I can see why you reacted the way you did." If it makes you feel better, you can also say, "I don't agree with the way you reacted, but I understand your point of view now."

- **Take responsibility for your part**. Even if your part in the argument was small, take responsibility for it. If you can do so sincerely, say you are sorry.

- **Accept any attempts your partner makes to repair things**. If your partner extends an olive branch, take it! This is not the time to be self-righteous, passive aggressive, or a victim. Open yourself up to any sincere gestures your husband extends toward you. Otherwise, you are teaching him that he shouldn't bother to make any reconciliation attempts with you in the future. Focus on the relationship, not on being right.

- **Learn and let go.** Come to some sort of resolution. Learn what you can and move on, truly leaving this particular disagreement behind you. Remember that research shows most disagreements in a relationship cannot be resolved, so deal with the ones most important to you, and understand that you may have to release the rest.

Negative events are inevitable and common in any relationship. You cannot be tuned into your spouse constantly, so there will be times when you misunderstand, hurt, or anger each other. Facing negativity together in a respectful manner is an incredibly powerful way to strengthen trust. Dealing successfully with conflict allows the two of you to move past the distressing event and can even bring you closer.

So, rather than running when there is any negativity, be courageous and embrace the opportunity to find some respectful resolution. This is especially important when the conflict is about something you value deeply.

BOTTOM LINE

Mismanaged conflict can kill a marriage.

Conflict will not kill a marriage, but you certainly can if you do not respond to conflict respectfully.

9

GIVE UP THE NAGGING BEHAVIORS THAT DRIVE YOU APART.

People are lonely because they
build walls, instead of bridges.
~Joseph Newton

A lthough mismanaged conflict can cause considerable damage to a marriage, there are many other chronic behaviors that can also insidiously undermine your relationship. Most people don't intentionally set out to hurt their spouse, but end up doing so anyway. Becoming conscious about how you interact with your partner puts you in the powerful position of choosing to actively foster the health of your marriage. All the little positive and negative things you do on a daily basis add up over time.

Lose the losing strategies.

If you recall, most men are incredibly sensitive to anything a woman says that could be construed as her telling him he is a failure, incapable, defective, weak, or just not measuring up. Giving "feedback," disagreeing, or pointing out that he was wrong about something can trigger a defensive reaction. Many women get irritated when men respond in this way, failing to understand a different approach is necessary. Renowned marital therapist Terrence Real, author of *The New Rules of Marriage*, notes that an important part of long-term successful engagement with a man involves giving up the following "losing" strategies that make it harder for him to let down his guard:

1. Needing to be Right.

When differences inevitably arise between you and your partner, it is easy to become trapped by the need to justify and defend your point of view or your way of doing things. The constant battling required for proving you are right hurts intimacy. Although it can be difficult to achieve, the focus needs to shift from "Who's right?" to acknowledging differences and negotiating the relationship.

2. Controlling your partner.

In an attempt to move toward a particular vision of how things "should be," many women become quite controlling in their relationships. You may want your husband to be the perfect host. You may want the house to be clean at all times. You may have a vision for how your birthday should be celebrated or how your husband should demonstrate his love on Valentine's Day. When these expectations are not met, many women become anxious and respond by exerting control, especially over their spouse. Remember that control is an illusion. You cannot really control your husband. If you try, he may appear compliant, but will typically feel resentful and suffocated, and may emotionally detach from you.

3. Unbridled self-expression.

There is a prevalent idea in American society that you should be 100% honest and open in a relationship. Some people consider this degree of openness an essential part of being authentic. Certainly, it is vital that you refrain from sweeping big problems under the rug. However, saying everything you think and feel, even if it is hurtful, is simply an excuse to be aggressive.

Emotionally composing yourself before you discuss touchy subjects is essential to protecting the respect in a relationship. It is easy to dismiss unkind, inconsiderate, or disrespectful things you do in a relationship by telling yourself, "I didn't really mean it." However, once it's all said or done, you can't take things back. So, rather than having regrets later, stop to think about how your partner might feel on the receiving end of any one of these behaviors before acting.

4. Withdrawal.

Pulling away from your partner takes many forms: surfing the Internet for hours, constantly working, having an affair, or not sharing your personal experiences. Excessive distance hurts the intimacy in a relationship, feeds resentment, and is often the first step toward giving up on a marriage. Sometimes withdrawal comes after you feel hurt. Other times, withdrawal on your part reflects your own difficulties with intimacy.

Don't let perfectionism convince you there is only one way to do things.

High-achieving women often define success as excelling, not just at work, but also in their personal lives. In her book, *The Type E* Woman: How to Overcome the Stress of Being Everything to Everybody*, psychologist Dr. Harriet Braiker portrays Type E women as:

- Striving for perfection and viewing anything less as a failure
- Having trouble relaxing if tasks are incomplete
- Trying to get more done in a day than is realistic
- Working to handle things on their own as much as possible
- Putting the needs of others ahead of their own

Living with someone who places high demands on themselves can be exhausting, especially if the intensity and stress of their life spills over into yours. Type E women often have trouble resting. When they are at work, they worry about tasks at home. When they are at home, their minds often wander off to unfinished business at the office. Women are still identified as the primary ones responsible for the home and children, so existing social pressure to manage these realms is compounded for high achievers. No high-achieving woman would want to be judged as a lousy housekeeper or mother!

Successful professional women are notorious for micromanaging and delegating to their husbands when they are on a mission to complete their never-ending "to do" list. If your husband does not understand why the items on your list are so important, he may become irritated and unhelpful. Because the social pressures on a man are different, he may have no idea why you are being so intense and may advise you to relax or drop certain tasks. A man is driven by his own mandate, which is to be tough, but not necessarily perfect. So, for example, during the holidays, when you insist the cards get out on time, and that the holiday gathering be coordinated in a certain way to capture the "magic of the season," he gets frustrated by all the demands you are making of him. The driver of this irritation is not that he doesn't want to help, but that that he doesn't get it.

Because men are expected to be invulnerable in the outside world, when they come home, they are often seeking refuge from the outer world and just want to relax. You, of course, want to relax too, but feel pressure to excel at your other roles. There are many "shoulds" running through your head: Your house *should* be homey; your children *should* always have nutritious, home-cooked meals; you *should* go visit that sick friend; and the list goes on. When your husband says, "I don't understand why everything is such a big deal," you feel more stressed and alone. The result is that you feel alienated from him, but still attempt to get your tasks done by intensifying your pace, micromanaging him, and ultimately feeling bitter about the responsibility you are carrying.

- "Don't forget that it's trash pickup tomorrow. Why don't you go ahead and put the trash out tonight?"
- "I need you to run to the store and get me some spaghetti sauce. Don't just grab any sauce. Get my favorite brand, or my whole dinner will be messed up."
- "The dishes will never come out clean if you load the dishwasher that way. Let me show you how to do it properly."
- "You need to cook the eggs longer; they're too runny. Also, don't put so much pepper on them next time."
- "Why don't you interact with the baby? Read her a book or tickle her tummy. She loves that."

You may just be trying to help by giving suggestions, but your husband may register your assistance as evidence that you believe he is incompetent and don't have faith in him. He may also feel disrespected if you fail to connect with him at a personal level before making any requests of him. Remember, stress can make you feel rushed, so you may get bossy and forget that simple things like eye contact, a considerate tone, and basic manners make a big difference. It's also easy to overlook the fact that as an independent adult, your husband has a right to say "no" to any request you make of him. If you ask a yes/no question, there are two possible answers. If only one is acceptable to you, it's important to look closer at your own behavior and expectations to see whether you are relating as an equal, or as a parent does to a child.

Deeply respecting the fact that your partner has different life experiences and his own ways of doing things is imperative. Although it may feel difficult, it is necessary for you back off and give him the space to approach tasks that he agrees to, using whatever process works for him. Just like when you are driving, there are many ways to get from Point A to Point B. Your way may be the best way for you. You will do much better with him if you are trusting and open to differences in how the two of approach the same tasks. He will also be more willing to help you in the specific way you want if you explain how his actions provide something you need (e.g., lowers your stress level, makes you feel loved, helps you get things done faster so you can relax together).

Burn the ownership papers.

A common, unspoken belief in many marriages is that you own each other. You may feel entitled to the love your spouse has to offer because you think that's what a husband is *supposed* to give you. This may seem obvious, but your husband is not "yours," even if you are legally married to him. You cannot force him to love you. You cannot make him care. If you approach your relationship with the entitled attitude that the he "owes" you love, you will be sadly disappointed at some point. This mindset actually kills affection.

Recognize that your partner *always* has complete freedom about loving you, and vice versa. A relationship continues because you repeatedly choose to stay with the person you love. You both stay because of how you feel in the connection with each other. If that feeling is positive, your partner will actually enjoy the commitment, and the odds of him wandering off decrease significantly. Don't take your husband's affection for granted, and make sure you behave in ways that invite connection.

This sense of entitlement can also extend to the little things both of you do on a regular basis. You may forget the value of what each of you does and come to expect the contribution your partner makes. For example, if your husband always fixes thing that are broken around the house, you may take this for granted. If you are the one paying the bills each month, your partner may assume that you will always meet this responsibility, and overlook the importance of this undertaking. Entitlement often shows up in statements such as:

He's my husband, so he should _____

I'm his wife, so I have a right to _____

I deserve _____

Entitlement often turns into demands, rather than requests. "You need to be at my office party next Friday," rather than, "There's an office party next Friday, and I'd love for us to go together. Can you make it?" If you want to get technical about it, being married does not mean that your husband must then comply with all your requests, and vice versa. As stated earlier, he has a right to say "no" to any request you make of him. You also have a right to agree or disagree with his response. Healthy relationships are negotiated. Entitlement and demands undermine the collaborative atmosphere necessary for fostering a vibrant marriage.

Don't let fear ruin your relationship.

Fear is one of your biggest enemies in a relationship. You may be scared that you will lose your partner, so you ask intrusive questions, keep tabs on where he is every minute, or become extremely jealous when he pulls away for any reason. He then thinks you don't trust him. You fear that he will not accept you as you are, so you hide out in the relationship. He then has difficulty connecting to you. You worry that you are not good enough, so you constantly seek reassurance. He becomes frustrated and exhausted by your never-ending insecurity.

Fear undermines love because when you are driven by fear, you will ultimately engage in actions that cause disconnection, and strain your love. Instead of finding ways to improve your marriage, your focus, instead, is on anticipating how your partner could hurt you, or exit the relationship. Ironically, this type of a relationship dance often creates the very situation you fear most.

You must find the courage to honestly evaluate whether your partner has the capacity to love you and honor his commitment to you. If you believe he does, use each new day to strengthen the connection between you. Don't let fear trick you into doubting your love if there is not any concrete reason to do so. You must give the relationship a real chance to thrive.

BOTTOM LINE

Everything you do and say counts.

A relationship can suffer "a death by a thousand cuts" if chronically harmful behavior is given free rein, as frequent hurtful actions will eventually rupture the deeper emotional bond in your marriage.

PART 4

THE INNER WORKINGS OF A DEEP AND PASSIONATE LOVE

Now that you know what *not* to do, in Part 4, we shift to the task of understanding how to actively build a marriage that endures the test of time. Social psychologist Dr. Elaine Hatfield distinguishes between passionate and companionate love. She defines passionate love as physical and emotional longing for someone. This is what you feel when you first fall in love. Companionate love, on the other hand, is less emotionally charged and characterized by an intimate friendship. The emotional environment of a relationship is vital to the survival of both types of love. Creating a steady partnership, while keeping passion alive, is not as natural as you would think, so let's explore the best ways to build the most fulfilling love possible.

10

PRACTICE SEVEN SIMPLE HABITS THAT MAKE LOVE LAST.

Trust love, even if it brings sorrow.
Do not close up your heart.
~Rabindranath Tagore

M any people believe that if you have truly found the right person, the relationship requires no effort to maintain at all. Working on your marriage then indicates there is something wrong, that perhaps you have fallen out of love. Relationships do require some investment of energy from time to time. For example, at the beginning of a marriage, it's not unusual to have to work on learning how to coexist peacefully. After all, you are two unique people with different upbringings, habits, values, and needs, attempting to share space and move your lives in unison. Major changes, such as the birth of a child or the death of a loved one, can also be times when your marriage requires attention. The Hollywood fantasy of being in love does not detail the real nuts and bolts of sustaining a relationship over the years.

The emotional environment the two of you create in your marriage has a tremendous effect on the strength of the connection between you. A strong emotional bond makes a marriage much easier to navigate, so deliberately working on creating an atmosphere that invites connection is vital to long-term relationship success.

People do not open up and bond on command. All of us are a bit like turtles: We can only be coaxed out of our shells when we are convinced it is safe to stick our necks out! Men, especially, through years of training, have become masterful at retreating. They are unlikely to risk vulnerability, unless there is a really good reason for doing so.

It is helpful to think of your relationship as a living thing that the two of you are growing in the space between you. Because it is alive, a relationship needs an interpersonal environment that is nurturing in order to flourish. Just as a plant needs nutrient-rich soil, water, sunshine, and space to grow, a relationship thrives on trust, respect, kindness, and appreciation. When a plant is generally well-cared-for, it is more likely to weather a storm and grow hardier over time.

And so it is with marriage. When the general climate is an emotionally-safe one, the bond grows deeper and more resilient over time. If, however, the emotional environment is threatening, most healthy people will default to protecting themselves over investing in the relationship, so the connection will ultimately suffer. In the worst case scenario, you end up with a marriage that is legally binding, but emotionally vacant.

There are certain relationship habits that keep the emotional environment conducive to protecting the steadiness and vibrancy of your marriage. Let's review some effective practices for helping a marriage thrive:

1. Generously infuse the relationship with positives.

Look around where you are right now. Notice everything in your surroundings that is the color blue. Got it? Now, <u>without</u> looking around again, I'd like you to list all the things you noticed that are green. What? You can't remember all of them? That means you are absolutely normal!

Your minds filter everything. From a cognitive standpoint, it is simply impossible for your brain to process every little tidbit of information that comes in through your senses. Even though filtering is necessary to prevent cognitive overload, sifting out these details is troublesome because it gives you skewed information, only part of the picture, so to speak. In your relationship, if you are feeling resentful of your spouse, you may lose track of the positive things he does because your brain is looking for information consistent with your negative view. The end result could be a highly inaccurate, distorted perception of your spouse, much like looking in a fun-house mirror.

Making a habit of noticing positives can do wonders to increase the warmth of your connection. In studying those he calls the Masters of Marriage (couples who have been married a long time and still like each another) vs. the Disasters of Marriage (those headed toward divorce), Gottman found that the Masters typically make about 20 positive statements for every negative one during their regular conversations with their spouse. In the midst of conflict, this ratio is reduced to 5:1, but is still well above the 1:1 of the Disasters group. So you can see that the Masters are extremely adept at keeping the relationship emotionally-warm and inviting. They express fondness, affection, and respect continuously.

We all love people who like us and make us feel good about ourselves. Think of a cherished person in your life, and I'll bet that person makes you feel special or valued. We also enjoy positive people who bring laughter and play into our lives, reminding us that life is not so bleak. Hopefully, you and your husband are still a source of positive feelings for each other. If not, don't despair. Just because things may be more negative now, does not mean that your marriage is necessarily doomed.

Most people are starving to be noticed and appreciated. Look for chances to express admiration, appreciation, and fondness to your spouse with comments such as the following:

- "You make me happy."
- "Thank you."
- "You are amazing."
- "I really love spending time with you."

- "I appreciate your taking care of me like you do."
- "I'm so lucky to be with you."
- "I trust you completely."
- "You're perfect for me."
- "I admire how you handled that situation."

A practical metaphor for tracking the positivity and negativity in your relationship is to think of the idea of an emotional bank account, a term used by John Gottman. Deposits include an attitude of generosity, compliments, acts of kindness, encouraging words, apologies, etc. Withdrawals include an attitude of entitlement, hurtful words, rejection, or callousness about your partner's needs.

Making emotional deposits on a regular basis, and truly accepting those made by your partner, is essential for the health of your marriage. If your spouse feels his actions always go unnoticed and unappreciated, he will feel frustrated and eventually stop doing his part, causing your relationship to spiral downward. Make it easy for him to please you, and you will see how much more he wants to give. If you cannot genuinely be positive toward your spouse right now, at least start by reducing the number of withdrawals, as that also improves your bottom line.

My 97-year-old grandmother used to wonder why people are so stingy with affection. She believed that there is an abundance of love in the world, and that we should extend it to others with tremendous generosity. She often wondered, "Why wouldn't you give away as much love as you can when it's free?" Wholeheartedly giving your affection, with no strings attached, is powerful. Ironically, your own heart will always be full when you love someone in this deeper way, and the good feelings between you will easily multiply.

2. Trust him.

Trust is built one experience at a time. Each time your partner is kind to you, listens attentively, and validates the real you, trust is built, brick by brick, one experience at a time. When trust breaks down, it leads to tremendous negativity. It's like a dam breaking open. When negativity floods a relationship, recovery can be difficult.

It is important to remember that no one is reliable 100% of the time. At some point, every person will disappoint or hurt you because no one is perfect. The deeper question you need to answer is whether you believe that your husband is as concerned about your well-being as he is his own. If your spouse has never given you any

145

concrete reason to mistrust him, give him the benefit of the doubt. When a person's words consistently line up with their actions, the odds are greater that they are trustworthy.

If the two of you are both committed to the marriage, acts of trust will typically steady you, and the trust will grow even deeper. Trust helps decrease reactivity by keeping you centered and grounded. When your husband wonders if you are truly there for him, make sure your behavior clearly reveals that the answer is a definite "yes."

3. Find him perfect, as is.

How deeply accepting are you of yourself and of your partner? Many men complain that women are always trying to change them. We even have a term for it: "husband training." Now I know everyone has to make some adjustments when they start living with their partner, but that's not what I'm talking about here. I'm referring to looking at your husband as if he were a never-ending project. Your mind gets fixated on all the things that need work. In the pursuit of perfection, you continually point out where he needs to target his energy. He gets the message that he is not good enough, and you lose sight of all his wonderful qualities: truly a lose/lose situation.

Meet your partner where he is today and work on lovingly accepting him "as is." Most women overestimate their spouse's level of confidence, assuming he has no insecurities and needs minimal validation. Acceptance is the first step in making him feel truly loved, respected, and affirmed. Yes, there may be some changes that you want to negotiate, but people are much more likely to work on improving themselves when they have deep acceptance, emotional regard, and encouragement from their partner. Giving someone a laundry list of all their faults and failures is usually not very motivating. Would that motivate you?

It is easier to accept your partner when you are actually tolerant of your own imperfections. When you judge yourself harshly and do NOT embrace your own vulnerabilities, you will probably be critical of your partner too. Or, if you truly feel you are not good enough, you may attempt to "sell" yourself to a man by making too many sacrifices and continuously showing him all the great things you can do for him.

Trust that your husband already recognizes your worth, and that you don't need to earn your value as a human being. Let your authentic self shine by respectfully expressing who you are, what you feel, and where you stand. If you need validation from you partner now and then, simply ask him, rather than indirectly seeking his approval. Try to find the courage to fully embrace both your humanity and his, understanding that every person has a need to feel valued and accepted exactly as they are.

4. Be kind.

Studies across cultures identify kindness as one of the top qualities people seek in a partner. Kindness, sincerity, and warmth are essential to helping you and your partner open up to each other. Treat yourself with kindness, as if you were your own best friend. Welcome interactions with gentleness, remembering the power you have to crush a person's spirit, even your own. We all want to feel treasured by the ones we love, so cherish your partner and let him know how much he means to you. A gentle, tender, and compassionate stance in relating to your partner does wonders for nurturing authenticity because you are making it safe for both of you to be yourselves.

5. Go with the flow.

Being fluid is another quality that is vital to the health of your marriage. The more rigid you are, the more likely you are to hurt the relationship. Life is complicated. People are complicated.

Things don't always go the way you want. Being adaptable keeps your relationship steady.

Choose to move into a cooperative stance in your marriage, avoiding power struggles that will clearly hurt your relationships. Although your spouse may do some things that drive you crazy, remember that you can cope. It is a waste of energy to struggle over every little thing. Learn to work together and trust each other, remembering you are on the same team and will both lose if you become overly rigid about little things.

Please note that it is difficult to "go with the flow" when you are not physically calm. Your ability to see the big picture becomes compromised by extreme stress or agitation. Knowing how to relax will deeply enhance your capacity for flexibility, so practice self-calming skills regularly to optimize your adaptability.

6. Be fair.

In the same way that the emotional bank account will register positive when there is sufficient emotional warmth in your relationship, a marriage will feel balanced when the two of you share responsibilities fairly. Social Exchange Theory says people look at the costs and benefits of being in a relationship. If they *perceive* that the actual benefits of being in the relationship consistently outweigh the costs, they stay in a relationship. If, however, they feel the scale is chronically tipped too much the other way, the exchange feels unfair, and the odds that they will end the relationship go up accordingly.

Resentment is one indicator that a person feels the relationship is unfair. When resentment builds up in a marriage, a couple often starts keeping tally of what each person is doing, a tit-for-tat situation. At the same time, they also stop acknowledging each other's positive contributions, causing the emotional bank account to start draining. "It's his job to mow the lawn every week. Why should I thank him for that? It's the least he can do. He never thanks me for the millions of things I do around here!"

Periodically check in with your partner to make sure things feel fair to both of you. If resentment starts building, do not address the issue by blaming your husband for the imbalance. Address it by negotiating for what you need. People often respond better when you appeal to a sense of fairness, than when you make demands or get angry. Work together until it feels as if both of you are contributing equally to the relationship and the burden on each of you is divided fairly. What is "equal" is a perception, so keep at it until you both agree responsibilities are distributed in a way that will not foster bitterness.

7. Guard respect above all.

No discussion about love is ever complete without talking about respect. Respect is the deep regard, appreciation, and valuing of a person. Respect is the very soil from which true love sprouts. In order for authenticity and deeper connection to emerge, the presence of respect is absolutely essential. When respect is lost, a healthy relationship is lost.

In many ways, respect is actually more important than love because if you have a deep respect for each other, you can usually rekindle feelings of love and passion, even if they wane for a while. Deeply-troubled relationships exhibit a tragic breakdown of respect. Domestic violence is the ultimate expression of complete disregard for a person's humanity. *When you behave in disrespectful ways toward your partner, you start to uproot the very essence of love.* For many people, respect is equated with love, so if they feel disrespected, they simultaneously feel unloved.

Sometimes people confuse respect and fear. For example, a parent might discipline a child harshly to get the child to "respect" them, but what actually emerges is fear. Respect is also confused with love. This is clear in a relationship where you have feelings of affection for someone, but treat each other poorly. When you have the deep conviction that you are worthy of being treated respectfully, you are much more likely to be intolerant of disrespectful behavior.

Respect is one of the things that cannot be compromised in a relationship. Respect must be consistently present and deeply anchored to keep love steady and strong over the long run. Respecting your partner is essential, as is respecting yourself. It is important to be clear about what you will or will not tolerate from your partner and to calmly guard the line of respect any time it is challenged. If you do not, this sets a dangerous precedent that may fuel more disrespectful interactions.

BOTTOM LINE

Love thrives in a positive environment.

Love grows best in an environment where there is deep trust, kindness, and respect. Dedicate yourself to behaving lovingly most of the time and doing your best to keep the atmosphere in your relationship as warm, loving, and positive as possible.

11

BUILD A DEEPLY INTIMATE FRIENDSHIP.

Chains do not hold
a marriage together.
It is threads,
hundreds of tiny threads
which sew people together
through the years
~Simone Signoret

Warmth and respect provide the ideal conditions for love to grow. Over time, the initial passion you feel for your partner will naturally evolve into a companionate love. Research clearly shows that when the foundation of a marriage is a deeply intimate friendship, that relationship can be tremendously rewarding and resilient in the face of life's hardships.

An intimate friend is very special because they really understand you, stand with you through hard times, and can be trusted with your deepest thoughts and feelings. Although your companion may not always agree with you, they hold you in high regard and do their best to support you. You genuinely respect and cherish each other, enjoy each other's company, and have an intimate knowledge of each person's unique likes and dislikes, hopes and dreams, and personality quirks.

Companionate love is at the heart of many successful marriages, but there is often a discrepancy between a person's *desire* for such a lasting, emotionally-close companionship and the actual *ability* to create it. This chapter explores the vital role of intimate friendship in a long-term relationship and reveals effective ways to build such a connection.

Three essential tools for creating intimacy

Simply living together does not guarantee that you and your partner will form an intimate friendship. Certainly, you learn many personal details about a person by sharing a home, as you become privy to daily routines, annoying habits, and general preferences. However, unless you make it a point to do so, you may never actually know each other's deepest fears, struggles, and dreams. It may not seem obvious, but you can be "together," but remain complete strangers to each other's internal worlds.

Intimacy has been described as "into-me-see," alluding to the transparency necessary to establish a deep emotional connection with another person. Although the need to be seen and understood is universal, it takes tremendous courage and trust to reveal your true self to someone. Intimacy deepens over time when openness is met with acceptance and caring.

Curiosity, deep listening, and empathy are three vital tools you can employ to enhance intimacy with your partner. Therapists routinely use these particular skills on a daily basis to discover the intimate details of people's lives. Let's examine each of these powerful tools more closely:

1. Curiosity

When your partner reacts more intensely than you believe the situation warrants, and the response makes no sense to you, your initial thought may be to assume that there is something wrong with him (e.g., "he's just a jerk"). That may be true, but it's also important to consider other potential reasons for his reaction. For example, if he gets mad when you call to find out why he's late, it's possible:

- His boss has been complaining about his being late to work. Now you've brought up the issue of his being late, and he feels defensive.
- He's sick and just grumpy.
- His mom was extremely controlling, and he is hypersensitive and overreacts to anything resembling how she behaved.
- He believes you are always complaining about him and is just really tired of it.
- He's emotionally immature and needs to grow up.
- He feels you don't trust him and are checking up on him.
- He's just having a really bad day and took it out on you.

As you can see, there are a variety of possible explanations, just for this one behavior! During a recent counseling session, I observed a woman become angry with her husband because he stopped holding her hand. She assumed he was upset about something she just said. When I pushed her to ask him why he had withdrawn his hand, he informed her that he had done so because his hand was sweaty! By the surprised look on her face, I could see this was not at all the response she had anticipated.

Women tend to make assumptions when their spouse becomes distant. Men often retreat when stressed, contemplating a problem, or needing some private time to refuel. It is important to learn what drives your partner to retreat. Without accurate knowledge, fear may convince you that your husband is hiding something or that he does not want to be with you. Try not to hunt down your partner, but rather, talk with him openly about what the space means. If you need reassurance, explain that to him, and ask him for support. After he has reassured you, you have to let go and trust, or risk damaging your connection.

Instead of assuming you know your partner so well that you can read his mind, consider the possibility that you actually can't. Instead, choose to step into a more inquisitive frame of mind. Be curious, not closed. Your initial hunch may be right, or you may be surprised to learn something new about what goes on in your husband's head.

2. Deep listening

Just as maintaining curiosity about your partner is important, but challenging, so is the act of listening deeply. Although we all enjoy the experience of having someone listen to us, we are not always good at providing that experience for others, especially those closest to us. When you have been in a relationship with someone for a while, it becomes harder to really listen to what they have to say. You may already think you know what your husband is going to say, so you only half-listen because you are a few steps ahead of him.

Many couples spend most of their time in conversation judging, mindreading, and rehearsing what they will say next; they rarely make a conscious effort to absorb what is truly communicated. Listening deeply means being curious and interested, keeping your own hot buttons in check, and making it your goal to clearly understand your spouse's perspective, whether or not you agree with how he sees things. If you honor your partner by listening deeply, you dramatically increase the chance you will learn his real view on things.

3. Empathy

Empathy is the ability to put yourself in someone else's shoes in an effort to imagine how things look and feel from their perspective. Most people want to feel understood, but it is the rare person that takes the time to appreciate the view from the other side of the fence. I wonder if you have ever considered what it is like to be in a relationship with you. Do you tend to be appreciative or critical? What do you think it's like for your partner when you express complaints? How about when you communicate appreciation and warmth?

Most of the time, when couples are talking, they are trying to convince each other that their way is the right one. It's like two people at a trial, presenting their cases before the judge. The end result is often gridlock. If you can shift into an empathic state and make an effort to hear his evidence, your partner will typically appreciate your efforts and eventually feel like you "get it." Even if the two of you don't agree, he will feel closer to you because of the consideration you have shown him.

Dig deeper, if he will allow it.

If you regularly engage your spouse with curiosity, deep listening, and empathy, it will be easier to get to know him better. The more you learn about your spouse's experiences, the more likely you are to understand his motivation, since we all relate to one another based on our life experiences and the lessons we gained from them. For example, knowing whether he came from a family that was comfortable with emotions is helpful. People who come from very emotionally-expressive families reveal their feelings with ease because that's what their families taught them. Others would rather have a tooth pulled than talk about their emotions because that's not something they are comfortable doing! Both types of people think they are "normal." However, if you and your spouse come from dissimilar backgrounds, there is greater risk of frequent misunderstandings. You would need to clearly understand, respect, and actively manage these differences.

Shifting communication to a level that elicits more intimate information is another way you can increase your understanding of your spouse. In his book *The Seven Levels of Intimacy: the Art of Loving and the Joy of Being Loved*, Matthew Kelly reveals how verbal communication affects the level of intimacy in our relationship. Keeping verbal communication more superficial keeps the relationship from deepening. Here is Kelly's list of the seven levels of communication, from least to most intimate:

1. **Cliches** (How are you? What have you been up to lately?)
2. **Facts** (What's the weather forecast? What did you do today?)

3. **Opinions** (What do you think about...? What do you prefer?)
4. **Hopes & dreams** (What are your goals for your life? What do you dream of doing?)
5. **Feelings** (What's the biggest hurt you've ever experienced in your life? What brings you joy?)
6. **Fears, failures, weaknesses** (What's your biggest fear? What do you feel you need to hide from others?)
7. **Needs** (What do you need to feel loved? What do you need to feel secure?)

Each level of communication serves a different purpose. Kelly notes that asking less-intimate questions is a good way to build rapport and determine whether it is safe to get closer to a person. So, although chatting with a stranger about the weather is not very intimate, it is certainly appropriate to the degree of closeness in that particular relationship. When people share low-risk information and are met with a positive response, they often become more willing to taking emotional risks in that relationship. They will watch closely to see if differences are accepted without judgment and criticism, and then typically put more and more on the line as emotional safety is established.

One powerful way to strengthen the intimate friendship in a marriage is to periodically venture to the deeper levels of communication. Occasionally ask your partner about his hopes and dreams for life, his daily struggles, and what he needs to feel fulfilled. Be willing to disclose the same information about yourself when the time is right.

Your success in building a more intimate connection is highly dependent on creating emotional safety. As a psychologist, my daily work is all about deliberately providing a relationship conducive to deep personal disclosure. I've had female clients who brought their husband into a session say, "I don't know what you did, but I've never heard him talk so much. I wish he would do that at home." All I did was intentionally create safe conditions for him to be open.

Although knowing the emotional highlights of your partner's inner life promotes compassion and understanding, do not forget that finding out such information is a privilege that is earned. *Being married does not entitle you to such information.* In fact, your husband may feel defensive or intruded upon if you suddenly start asking many probing questions. On the other hand, he could also be highly touched that you want to know more about him. Every person has different privacy boundaries, and it is necessary to respect any limits your partner imposes on the amount of information he wants to disclose *and* the pace at which he does so. If you are too pushy, impatient, or entitled, you may unintentionally damage, not strengthen, your relationship.

Some people are simply not comfortable with verbal communication and self-disclosure, so you may need to rely on other ways to deepen your bond. Although most women routinely talk as a way to establish connection, a majority of men need to feel connected with their partner *before* they engage in intimate verbal communication.

Because anything unfamiliar takes energy, people who don't typically relate at a deeper level sometimes find such conversations exhausting and uncomfortable. It may be unrealistic and unnecessary to constantly delve into the most intimate levels of communication. Having fewer intimate conversations does not doom your marriage, as you are not trying to perfectly map every detail of your husband's psychological landscape! Remember, the goal is actually to get an *adequate* glimpse of each other's true selves and to create relationship conditions that invite more authentic interaction, at whatever pace the two of you can handle.

Unload the emotional baggage.

In the early months of the relationship, it is very difficult to know how your partner typically relates. That's because research shows that when you first fall in love with someone, there are powerful hormones in your bloodstream that literally alter your brain chemistry, leading you to idealize your partner and feel addicted to him! Lust, attraction, and desire are strong, causing both of you to be more open and emotionally available than usual. It's not until the hormone levels go down, about 18-24 months later, that you start to get insight into your partner's true relational style.

Noted marriage therapist, Dr. Harville Hendrix, author of *Getting the Love You Want*, says that once the honeymoon phase ends, people start to unpack their emotional baggage and reveal clues to their true selves. At this point, many relationships end because their partners don't like what they see. Hendrix warns that the honeymoon phase always ends. He suggests that partners help one another sort through the emotional baggage they brought with them so they can create a more intimate and rewarding relationship.

One fruitful area to explore, if your spouse is receptive, is his prior experience with other important relationships. Our families teach all of us our first lessons about trust, vulnerability, autonomy, emotional expression, sexuality, and personal worth. People who grew up in households where parents were responsive, reliable, and caring often come to expect that the world is a safe place where people can be trusted. On the contrary, people whose caregivers were extremely harsh, inconsistent, or simply absent, learn the opposite. If a person has never known how it feels to have someone reliably meet their physical and emotional needs, he may feel unsafe, struggle with insecurity, and strongly resist getting too close to anyone. I have worked with several individuals whose parents were extremely critical or abusive. These individuals had to learn how to trust in the safety of a therapeutic relationship before they could do so in their marriages.

Relationships with siblings, friends, grandparents, teachers, coaches, bosses, children, and romantic partners also shape our view of interpersonal connection. For example, being cherished by a favorite grandparent can increase your sense of self-worth in a relationship. Harmful experience, like being an outcast in high school, abused by a parent, or betrayed by an ex may lead to feelings of fear about connection. When there is a close emotional bond and a safe, loving environment in a marriage, a person can know the true power of being seen and cherished by another human being, and this can be truly life-altering.

Once again, remember that most healthy people will not engage at a deeply-intimate level of communication until it is absolutely clear that it is emotionally safe to do so. Emotional intimacy is highly dependent on trust. If you are usually critical, dismissive, or confrontational when your partner discloses, the door to more intimate communication may already be closed with a giant padlock. Obtaining answers to deeply personal questions may be unrealistic, unless damage to feelings of safety or trust is first repaired.

Spot the ways he is already telling you he loves you.

The connection with your spouse deepens when your spouse behaves lovingly. Since the majority of women rely on verbal communication to deepen emotional intimacy, they may be looking for words like, "I love you" or "I can't live without you" as evidence of their partner's affection for them. Men, especially those not as comfortable with verbal intimacy, may build interpersonal intimacy in other ways, such as spending time together or being helpful. Flirting, humor, and gifts can all communicate a desire for closeness. Your partner may connect with you by completing your honey-do list, cleaning out your car, or initiating sex. He may compliment you, support your dreams, and prioritize you in his life to show you what you mean to him. He may feel completely misunderstood and hurt when your response is to tell him he's selfish and doesn't care about you because he won't have a deep conversation with you.

Remember that when most men visit with their male friends, they often go out and do something together, rather than have long chats. In fact, I remember a client telling me her husband had recently enjoyed a four-hour road trip with his best friend, and that he and his buddy remained silent the entire time. It's hard to imagine two female friends being quiet for that long! Although it may feel strange to do so, open yourself up to the possibility of doing enjoyable things together as a way of getting closer.

Just being in close proximity can engender feelings of connection in men, which is why a man may feel you've both shared an intimate time when you watched a movie together. You, on the other hand, may want to talk about the movie (and many other things!) to feel a real connection has happened. Physical intimacy is also a part of maintaining a healthy emotional connection with your spouse, especially if he is not much of a talker. Physical affection and sex can be powerful demonstrations of emotional closeness and trust.

Keep your eyes open for the range of ways your partner may be trying to emotionally connect with you. Even if you don't consistently hear the words, "I love you," he may actually be expressing such feelings to you frequently through his actions. Make sure you notice.

Don't let the intimate connection unravel.

As the years go by, especially after children enter the family, the intimate friendship between partners can become strained. Women often lose themselves in the demands of work, marriage, and motherhood, leaving little of their original selves for their husbands to love. When you spend less time together because you are busy, it's easy to feel neglected.

The sexual connection with a spouse can unravel, as getting a good night's sleep, work demands, or tending to young children trump the desire for sexual intimacy. For many women, self-consciousness about physical appearance or lack of emotional intimacy strongly affects their willingness to engage sexually. Unfortunately, the less a couple has sex, the less likely they are to have sex in the future; truly a "use it or lose it" situation which results in some individuals being in a sexless marriage. Although sex is an important form of emotional connection for men and women, more often than women, men rely on sex as evidence of their partner's deep desire, acceptance, and love.

When a couple no longer connects physically, feelings of rejection can compromise their emotional connection further. Someone who becomes emotionally disconnected from their partner may stray outside the relationship. A prevalent myth in the culture is that men are obsessed with sex and will step outside their marriage whenever the opportunity presents itself. In reality, the number-one reason men and women become involved in affairs is emotional dissatisfaction with their marriage. Research shows that emotional affairs are actually on the rise. In this type of affair, there is no physical intimacy, but there is a close and meaningful emotional connection. Any type of affair signals clearly that a marriage is struggling.

The work of researchers John Gottman, Caryl Rusbult, and Shirley Glass has been used to develop a model of how betrayal unfolds in a relationship. What they refer to as the "Cascade of Betrayal" begins when one of you feels the other is not really looking out for your best interests anymore. Trust begins to break down and you start to turn away from the relationship. Then, conflict and negativity increase, leading to the relationship becoming mired in feelings of contempt. Obviously, hostility does not feel good, so both of you start to avoid the tension by keeping more and more of your real thoughts from each other in order to reduce the chances of an argument.

Feeling unloved, unappreciated, and inadequate, you resign yourself to the conviction that your partner is selfish and does not care about you anymore. Resentment builds and the level of loneliness in the relationship rises considerably. If you are the distressed partner, you start to contemplate whether you can, "do better than this" and your investment in the relationship drops considerably. You become convinced that you cannot make your partner happy, enter a disempowered state, and withdraw emotionally. Energy gets redirected toward hiding out, appearing unaffected, or simply trying not to upset your partner. Eventually you stop seeking connection with your partner altogether and begin confiding in people outside the relationship. For both men and women, loss of emotional intimacy will typically also lead to loss of desire for sexual connection. At some point, you start to cross boundaries and actively turn toward others to meet your deeper emotional needs, allowing real betrayal to unfold.

Although many marriages do survive an affair, rebuilding a marriage where trust has been violated requires tremendous courage, commitment, and hard work. Preventing a relationship from unraveling to the point that one party is having an affair saves considerable heartache. Contrary to popular opinion, men are perfectly capable of commitment and fidelity and will freely commit to a woman who generates positive feelings, believes in him, and makes life easier. He will want both sexual and emotional closeness with her if she respects, values, and appreciates him deeply.

Keep learning about each other.

It is important to protect and nurture the health of the underlying intimate connection through the variety of ways discussed in this chapter. Take the time to continue learning about each other, remembering that everyone makes sense once you know their history...everyone. Openly share the challenges and joys of life, but also remember that other forms of intimacy can be powerful in generating warm feelings between you and your partner. Sharing a good laugh, as well as doing something new, fun, or relaxing together, can all increase emotional connection. And sometimes, a look or a touch at just the right time can speak volumes.

The deep intimacy of companionate love can keep your marriage strong and allow you to relax and direct your energy to other things. However, remember that it can be a short distance from comfort to boredom or from familiarity to lack of appreciation. In the next chapter, we explore the reality of passionate love and what is required to sustain it beyond the first few years in a relationship.

BOTTOM LINE

Deep intimacy binds you together.

The strongest marriages are based in deep friendship. The better you know each other, the deeper the understanding and emotional bond between you. Will you take the risk to let yourself be known? It's up to you. The difference between a "yes" and "no" can be the difference between an emotionally-intimate or lonely marriage.

12

KEEP PASSION ALIVE.

The first kiss is magic.
The second is intimate.
The third is routine.
~Raymond Chandler

R elationships that last more than a couple of years face unique obstacles. Contrary to popular opinion, even people with great marriages, who are able to easily sustain emotional closeness, may find it difficult to keep the passion in their marriages alive. Dr. Sonja Lyubomirsky, author of *The Myths of Happiness*, notes that research across cultures consistently shows that the intense longing, desire, and attraction of passionate love are typically replaced by the deep affection and connection of companionate love within two years. Although this progression is quite normal, many people feel quite disappointed when deep desire plummets, and begin to question whether there is something wrong with their marriage or partner.

Habituation is the enemy.

Why is it difficult to sustain passion indefinitely? Is there anything you can do to get passion back after the two years are up? Or, do you simply need to accept that having a really close companion you love is the most you can hope for in the long run? Let's begin by understanding the main reason that passionate love is elusive for so many people.

In her book, *Mating in Captivity,* psychotherapist Esther Perel, notes that *the very conditions that nurture a deep, steadfast love are actually the same ones that kill passion*! Familiarity, security, and routine inspire companionship, emotional intimacy, and affection, but desire is actually ignited by polar opposite conditions, such as novelty, surprise, and emotional space.

The reason the passion of new love is physically and practically impossible to maintain in the long term is because of habituation. Habituation refers to the tendency of your brain to respond less and less to something you are exposed to repeatedly. For example, you might habituate to the sound of the air conditioner in your house because it's always in the background. In a relationship, over time, you become less likely to notice and appreciate your partner because you are always around each other. Familiar things literally become less noticeable because the human brain is designed to respond primarily to novelty. So, even if you are passionately in love with someone, your brain gets used to that feeling, dials it down, and moves on to newer things eventually.

Although habituation may be the enemy of passion, it is actually a source of tremendous comfort in a relationship too. Knowing you can rely on your partner to be there day after day provides a sense of emotional security and allows you to relax. Routines, as boring as they may seem, help keep stress levels down.

That being said, a relationship can become completely uninspiring and downright boring if nothing ever changes. Huge disappointment can result when a person feels their marriage is like Groundhog Day and can't even see what's so special about their partner anymore. Habituation must be actively managed because it can easily destroy attraction, passion, and the overall quality of the relationship.

Despite the low odds of staying in an intensely passionate state forever, it is possible for relationships to sustain an element of desire. In the same way that you can strengthen the deeper connection of intimate friendship, there are ways to intentionally rekindle passion within a committed relationship.

The specific conditions that ignite passion

Many people mistakenly think passion is just about sex. It is not. If you are a passionate person, this can certainly enhance your sex life, but passion is really about the emotional energy you bring to the connection. Being relaxed, intriguing, positive, and lighthearted naturally engenders passion. Pulling away for a while, then fully reengaging, creates some intrigue and positive tension. Passionate sex happens when you have emotional intimacy in a relationship, paired with playfulness and a sense of adventure.

Most people don't usually think of planning and passion as going together, but being intentional in your pursuit of more passion is important, especially the longer you are married. Rekindling passion is largely about reintroducing some of the original conditions, such as space, novelty, and fun, that fed the intense feelings. Most people want their partner to see them as special and irresistible, so restoring passion is primarily about keeping yourself interesting and approaching your spouse in an emotionally-provocative way.

Let's review some of the more potent ways you can deliberately make it easier for passion to reemerge in your marriage:

1. Have enough breathing room

In a healthy relationship, you have a capacity to connect deeply, but also tolerate separation. If you remember that a relationship is a living thing, you will then understand that if you hold on too tightly to it, you will literally suffocate it to death. Loving is a delicate balance of holding on and letting go, of closeness and space. *Passion thrives in the space.* Think of the last time your spouse went on a trip and how you felt when he returned. Did you see him any differently when he got back? Distance often allows for a sense of mystery to emerge and anticipation to build, making it more likely you will experience more intense feelings like longing.

People vary in the amount of togetherness and space they need. Some couples do most things together, while others have essentially separate lives that overlap at certain points in the day. What matters most is that the two of you agree on how much closeness and distance work for you, and that the underlying emotional connection remains steady and strong. Just remember that the type of connection you develop depends on what you are nurturing. If passion is what you want more of, you could try spending some time apart to see if that helps. If you and your spouse value constant companionship over passion, then having time away from each other may not matter so much.

Freedom must be present in a relationship for it to remain alive. People like to come and go as they please, within reason, of course. They also need to know you can survive without them, so being independent and non-possessive is vital. With the movement toward and away from each other, you can bring in interesting things from your separate lives. Remember not to squeeze too tightly! Practice a degree of healthy detachment. Intimate separateness is the goal. Allow the relationship as much breathing room as you can handle, without disappearing emotionally.

The most important thing is that you have your own life! Being in your own zone can be a turn-on. When your partner gets a little distance and has a fresh view of your radiance and self-confidence, this certainly can stir up some passion!

2. Keep things interesting.

Novel, challenging, stimulating activities can infuse new life into a stagnating relationship. If you want the relationship to be a source of long-term enjoyment and fulfillment, make sure you are growing both individually and together.

When you are learning new things and maturing over time, this makes you more interesting and fresh in your partner's eyes. Research by Dr. Aron and Gary W. Lewandowski Jr. has found that when a person is able to expand their knowledge and experiences through the relationship, a process they call "self-expansion," they are much more satisfied with and committed to the relationship. Introducing new friends, discussing an interesting news story, or taking a weekend away to a new place can enhance satisfaction in the relationship.

Many couples with long-standing relationships fall into a rut, always doing the same things. Life gets serious and boring, with most of their time revolving around responsibilities and obligations. You both need to have fun! The problem is that what is fun to you, may not be fun to your spouse. Openness is required to discover new ways to play together. He may want to watch a movie; you may want to go dancing. It's helpful if each of you creates a list of activities you like to do or would like to try. Take turns introducing each other to new things you would not normally pursue. When it comes to novelty and variety, your interpersonal differences may actually be a huge asset, if you keep an open mind.

3. Be present

When you engage your husband, how many times are you *really* there? How often do you stop what you are doing to listen to what he's saying? Are you usually absorbed in the moment when having sex, or just waiting for it to be done?

One of the great drivers of passion is being fully present in the moment. Full engagement through eye contact, passionate kissing, or slow, sensual touch gets the attention of most partners! One of the deepest needs of a human being is to be "seen" by another. When that happens, desire can intensify, especially when there is a loving and accepting environment.

When paired with a strong, emotional connection, more lighthearted qualities work their own magic to reignite passion. Flirting, teasing, and whispering sweet nothings demonstrate confidence, which most people enjoy. Laughter, joyfulness, and relaxation are also alluring. People are drawn to all these qualities because they make us feel so alive.

Tend to the spark and learn to fan it.

You cannot sustain passion by letting things happen naturally because the larger social environment harms passion. Passion is like a fire that you must attend to regularly, or it will go out. The idea of being deliberate in keeping the passion in your marriage is not a romantic one for most people, but is the only way to keep passion alive over the long run.

Think back to when you first met your husband. Part of what drew you to him was that he was a stranger, someone new and mysterious you took great pleasure in discovering. Because your lives were clearly separate, there was emotional and physical space between you. This made it much easier for you to fantasize about him, long for him, and admire him from a distance. When you did get together, chances are that, at first, you regularly did things that were interesting or fun. Fast forward to now...are you still doing any of these things?

If your answer is "no," you are like most people...and have some work to do.

BOTTOM LINE

Passion dies unless it is deliberately sustained.

Passion thrives when there is space, novelty, fun, surprise, adventure, humor, playfulness, and creativity. Deliberately cultivate these qualities at times you want to reignite the spark of passion.

PART 5

PROTECTING LOVE

Armed with an understanding of what threatens and strengthens a relationship, let's now examine long-term strategies for protecting your marriage from outside forces. Designing a lifestyle conducive to relationship health requires a few additional skills and a willingness to make tough choices. Making lifestyle changes can sometimes be challenging, especially if your life is chaotic. However, the reward of doing so is that the odds of your marriage suddenly taking a nosedive are minimized, and you can shift into maintenance mode, which requires significantly-less effort.

13

DESIGN A LIFESTYLE THAT KEEPS LOVE STRONG.

Any intelligent fool
can make things bigger,
more complex, and more violent.
It takes a touch of genius
and a lot of courage to
move in the opposite direction.
~E.F. Schumacker

Y‌ou have been provided with a clear, potent roadmap for building a successful relationship. To help you stay focused on what is most important, here is a brief review of the actions that will give you the greatest return on your investment of time and energy:

1. **Strengthen yourself first.** Work on identifying your needs, and take responsibility for getting them met. Make

yourself a clear priority in your life, recognizing that unless you develop a strong sense of self, your relationship will probably continue struggling.

2. **Strengthen the positive climate of your relationship**. Stop engaging negatively, and deliberately relate to your partner in ways that clearly convey your deep regard for him.

3. **Choose to operate out of love, courage, and trust.** Start with the assumption that your husband loves you, needs you, and wants your marriage to work as much as you do.

4. **Create conditions that increase intimacy with your partner.** Prioritize spending more time with each other, and strengthen the intimate friendship between you, using the strategies outlined in this book. This deep bond is ultimately what will keep you together, even through hardship.

5. **Keep your focus and persist.** When you forget where you are going, come back to the information here, and regroup. Be willing to seek professional help if necessarily, and remind yourself not to give up. Persistence, not perfection, will typically pay off!

There is one more step necessary for long-term relationship success: You must create an environment that shelters your relationship, so it can continue growing without the need for constant intervention. If not, even when you have a strong sense of self and are mindful of your actions, your marriage can perish in the face of unyielding outside forces. No matter how strong the sailboat or skilled the sailor, if a ship is constantly being tossed about on a turbulent sea, it will eventually be damaged, and may sink. Because the environment is a constant source of potential threat to a relationship, one imperative for protecting marriage is to deliberately design a lifestyle that shelters it.

Making lifestyle changes can feel intimidating, especially when you are living your life at a hectic pace. However, like any other change, modifying your way of life is achieved by taking small steps in the direction you desire. You have to identify your top life priorities, and then choose your way to relationship success.

Figure out your "Big Rocks."

Author Stephen Covey's story of the "Big Rocks in Life" illustrates the process of prioritizing what is important to you. Covey points out that if you pack a large container up to the top with fist-sized rocks, the container will look full. Look closer and you will see space to add smaller rocks, gravel, and sand. Full now? No. You can add water which can seep into more of the space. Life is like that container; you can easily fill it up with small, unimportant stuff, leaving very little room for the big rocks, the priorities you hold most dear. Covey's point is that you must make room for the big rocks first, or you will never have room for what you value most. If you want your marriage to survive in the midst of constant social pressure, it <u>must</u> be one of your big rocks.

In this society, many people are constantly seeking to have it all, without ever defining "IT" clearly. As a result, unfocused busyness clutters your ability to discern what's truly important to you. Precious time and energy are wasted on things you would rather not do and with people you don't even enjoy, while what you love most gets lost in the shuffle. You cannot achieve your dreams unless you realistically identify them, and put them at the center of your life.

A speech given by Brian Dyson, a former CEO of Coca-Cola Inc., eloquently describes what is at stake when we are not clear about what matters in life:

Imagine life as a game in which you are juggling some five balls in the air. You name them—work, family, health, friends and spirit—

and you're keeping all of these in the air. You will soon understand that work is a rubber ball. If you drop it, it will bounce back. But the other four balls—family, health, friends and spirit— are made of glass. If you drop one of these, they will be irrevocably scuffed, marked, nicked, damaged or even shattered. They will never be the same. You must understand that and strive for Balance in your life.

Simplify

Simplifying your life is one way to make sure your time is focused on what you hold most dear and brings you the most satisfaction, like your marriage. If keeping your marriage strong is a key priority, you must start stepping away from the forces in your life that jeopardize your relationship. For example, if your works demands too much travel, perhaps you need to find another job. If all your spare time is dedicated to optional activities that leave little time with your spouse, you must decide how much your marriage matters.

Even if you have your priorities straight, the minutia of life can still drain your energy and resources. In keeping with Stephen Covey's analogy, definitely put the big rocks in your bucket first, but also limit how much gravel, sand, and water you add. Otherwise, you will end up with a very heavy bucket that is burdensome to carry around!

Applying the Pareto Principle ensures your time and energy are being channeled in the ways you value most. The 80/20 Principle, first stated by Vilfredo Pareto in 1897, says that 20% of our effort produces 80% of the results, so that 80% of our effort produces very little result. Here are a few examples of this principle:

- 20% of the things in your house are used 80% of the time
- 80% of the things in your house are used 20% of the time
- 20% of your relationships give you 80% of your satisfaction
- 20% of the members of an organization do 80% of the work
- 20% of the books in a bookstore account for 80% of the sales.

Pareto's Principle has been used for decades to streamline business efficiency and can be applied to your personal life to purge clutter, improve relationships, and reduce information overload. If your life is not as you want it, analyze where your energy is going and then redirect it to the activities and relationships that matter to you most.

Nurture your most important relationships, and stop investing in the rest. Identify your most important valuables, and get rid of what is just taking up space. Skip over the 80% of useless information coming into your life, and find the 20% that is actually important. The challenge is to recognize the 20% of vital items, activities, and relationships that add the most to your life, so you can emphasize them over the 80% that just blocks you from getting what you want. As you let go of what drains you, you will free up energy to dedicate to your marriage.

Share responsibilities.

Most people do not want to spend their spare time scrubbing the bathtub, grocery shopping, or pulling weeds. Yet, no matter how much anyone simplifies their life, mundane tasks remain, using up precious time and energy that could be spent on more important matters. Leveraging your financial and personal resources to eliminate these routine tasks from your "to do" list is one effective way to create more space for your priorities.

Your tendency may be to always say, "I can do it myself." However, if you are serious about having balance in your life, ask yourself, "Am I the only one who can take care of this chore?" If the answer is "no," it may make much more sense to delegate the task. Enlisting the help of other people or technology can significantly decrease the constant time pressure you feel. Consider some of the following changes:

- Ask your children to assume responsibility for feeding the dogs, taking dirty clothes to the laundry room, and keeping their rooms clean.
- Set up automated bill-pay services.
- Hire a housekeeper to come in twice a month to do detail cleaning.
- Join, or create, a neighborhood carpool with parents of kids attending your child's school.
- Buy a programmable vacuum cleaner that operates automatically while you are away.
- Use a lawn service to keep the outside of your home well-kept.
- Negotiate with your spouse to take on additional responsibilities.

Focusing your own energy primarily on what actually *requires* your direct involvement can be an excellent way to keep lifestyle-related stress manageable. Although you may initially feel guilty for handing over tedious tasks to someone else, you and your relationships will benefit tremendously from the breathing room you gain.

<u>BOTTOM LINE</u>

It is important to design a lifestyle that protects your relationship.

All the hard work of strengthening yourself and your marriage is in jeopardy as long as your relationship is chronically exposed to a harmful environment. Identify your marriage as a priority, and then design a lifestyle that keeps love strong.

14

WHEN THE GOING GETS TOUGH

Do you want me to tell you
something really subversive?
Love is everything
it's cracked up to be.
That's why people are
so cynical about it.
It really is worth fighting for,
being brave for,
risking everything for.
And the trouble is,
if you don't risk anything,
you risk even more.
~Erica Jong

T he choice to be a steadfast companion on life's journey is an act of courage and hope. Life holds many surprises, and it is difficult to know how each challenge you encounter will affect your marriage. Facing increasing doubt that you can continue to walk together is painful. The best you can do is move forward wholeheartedly, with emotional courage, a clear head, and a commitment to doing your best.

Have the courage to surrender to the change process.

Even courageous people feel scared when facing difficulty. Courage is the willingness to accept that fear is a part of life and taking a step in the desired direction anyway. The natural tendency is to cling to the banks of the river when you really need to let go and trust that the water will ultimately carry you to a greater destiny. If you surrender yourself to slowly altering what is not working in your relationship, you will typically end up in a more positive place.

Permanent change does take time, and it is easy to become impatient with the process, especially when you are emotionally struggling in a difficult marriage. Most people assume change is a straight line from the point you make a decision to the point where you reach your goal. In fact, change is more like the stock market graph. There are many ups and downs, but if you are generally headed in a positive direction, you will succeed. *Again, perseverance, not perfection, is the key. Choosing love over fear repeatedly is necessary.*

Choose to move toward him.

A marriage does not remain healthy and survive hardship by chance. Instead, such longevity is the result of thousands of decisions to move *toward* your partner, rather than away, especially when things are tough.

You may truly believe that your relationship can never get better because you see your husband drifting away from you, and you're convinced he doesn't care for you any longer. You may assume the solution is to try to get him to change course. You're right, if he would take some steps toward you, it could improve your relationship. However, the problem with framing your marital difficulties in this way is that it renders you powerless. You are completely at the mercy of your husband's decisions.

Never forget, <u>you</u> can also move closer to him, and that doing so is much more under your control than trying to get him to change. Consider taking some of the following steps toward your partner to clearly signal your commitment to strengthening your love:

- Reach out when your partner is hurting.
- Be willing to say "I'm sorry" first.
- Take the job that allows you the most flexibility.
- Assume additional responsibilities when your spouse is overwhelmed.
- Call your mother-in-law because your husband loves her.
- Listen without judging your partner.
- Seek help for behaviors that harm your relationship (e.g., addiction, abuse).
- Don't reciprocate someone's obvious romantic interest in you.
- Be kind when your partner is having a bad day.
- Get a babysitter, and go out on a real date
- Believe your husband when he says he loves you and is committed to the relationship.

As Maya Angelou says, "When you know better, you do better," meaning that even if you have made mistakes in the past, you now have the power to make better choices. Use the information here as a roadmap. Study it. Apply it. And take note of what happens. Have the courage to be the bigger person and to bridge the distance between you and your husband, so you can build a resilient and rewarding marriage.

Above all, never underestimate your power as an agent of change. Often, all it takes is one individual, leading with courage and determination, to get the relationship moving in a much healthier direction.

BOTTOM LINE

Choosing love over fear keeps love strong.

Have the courage to choose love again and again to keep your marriage strong.

APPENDIX A

SUMMARY OF
BOTTOM LINES

❖ **The modern environment makes it harder to navigate a relationship.**
The social environment perpetuates fear, confusion, and bad advice about relationships. You must develop a solid understanding of how to keep a relationship healthy and maintain a courageous mindset capable of defeating the unrelenting forces that threaten a marriage.

❖ **All of us have a need to be understood, appreciated, and cherished.**
Men and women may seem quite different from one another. Although there is much confusion about gender roles and whether men and women differ in their capacities for engagement at a more intimate level,

remember that we are all human and have similar core emotional needs.

❖ **Stress can be toxic to a relationship.**
Chronic activation of the body's hardwired stress response poses a threat to relationships. When a person is highly stressed, they do not function in ways that support the relationship. You must proactively manage outside pressures on your relationship in order to cultivate a healthful environment that makes it easier for love to grow. Respecting personal limits and making choices that allow you to function within those limits are vital to managing stress.

❖ **The ability to calm yourself is essential to full engagement with your spouse.**
Stress makes it tremendously difficult to connect with your partner in a constructive way. Mastering self-calming skills and having appropriate expectations of your spouse are essential to both personal and relationship health.

❖ **True change begins the moment you embrace truth.**

The kind of love most people long for takes tremendous courage and personal responsibility to attain. Dare to open yourself up to the change process by removing your personal barriers to change so you can move your relationship in a more positive direction.

❖ **A strong sense of self is essential to a healthy marriage.**

A man is not there to "complete" you. Unless you have a strong, separate sense of self, it is virtually impossible to sustain a healthy love that remains steady over time.

❖ **Your authentic self is irresistible.**

From the moment you were born, the world began to define who you are, how you should live, and what you must do to be accepted. With all this external influence, it is easy to lose touch with your authentic self. No one can love you if you are not even present. Showing up as yourself in the relationship and engaging in loving action makes you irresistible.

❖ **Mismanaged conflict can kill a marriage.**
Conflict will not kill a marriage, but you certainly can if you do not respond to conflict respectfully.

❖ **Everything you do and say counts.**
A relationship can suffer "a death by a thousand cuts" if chronically harmful behavior is given free rein, as frequent hurtful actions will eventually rupture the deeper emotional bond in your marriage.

❖ **Love thrives in a positive environment.**
Love grows best in an environment where there is deep trust, kindness, and respect. Dedicate yourself to behaving lovingly most of the time and doing your best to keep the atmosphere in your relationship as warm, loving, and positive as possible.

❖ **Deep intimacy binds you together.**
The strongest marriages are based in deep friendship. The better you know each other, the deeper the understanding and emotional bond between you. Will you take the risk to let yourself be known? It's up to you. The difference between a "yes" and "no" can be

the difference between an emotionally-intimate or lonely marriage.

❖ **Passion dies unless it is deliberately sustained.**
Passion thrives when there is space, novelty, fun, surprise, adventure, humor, playfulness, and creativity. Deliberately cultivate these qualities at times you want to reignite the spark of passion.

❖ **It is important to design a lifestyle that protects your relationship.**
All the hard work of strengthening yourself and your marriage is in jeopardy as long as your relationship is chronically exposed to a harmful environment. Identify your marriage as a priority, and then design a lifestyle that keeps love strong.

❖ **Choosing love over fear keeps love strong.**
Have the courage to choose love again and again to keep your marriage strong.

APPENDIX B

RECOMMENDED READING

Relationships

Getting the Love You Want: A Guide for Couples, 20th Anniversary Edition, Harville Hendrix. Henry Holt & Co., 2007

How to Improve Your Marriage without Talking about It, Patricia Love & Steven Stosny. Three Rivers Press, 2008.

Marriage Rules: A Manual for the Married and Coupled Up, Harriet Lerner. Gotham, 2012.

Mating in Captivity: Unlocking Erotic Intelligence, Esther Perel. Harper Perennial, 2007.

The Dance of Intimacy: A Woman's Guide to Courageous Acts of Change in Key

Relationships, Harriet Lerner. William Morrow, 1990.

The New Rules of Marriage: What You need to Know to Make Marriage Work, Terrence Real. Ballantine Books, 2008.

The Seven Principles for Making Marriage Work: A Practical Guide from the Country's Foremost Relationship Expert, John M. Gottman & Nan Silver. Three Rivers Press, 2000.

We Love Each Other, but...Simple Secrets to Strengthen Your Relationship and Make Love Last, Ellen F. Wachtel. St. Martin's Griffin, 2000.

Gender Differences

Gendered Lives: Communication, Gender, and Culture, Julia T. Wood. Cengage Learning, 2010.

Pink Brain, Blue Brain: How Small Differences Grow Into Troublesome Gaps—and What We Can Do About It, Lise Eliot. Mariner Books, 2010.

Real Boys: Rescuing Our Sons from the Myths of Boyhood, William Pollack. Owl Books, 1999.

Reviving Ophelia: Saving the Selves of Adolescent Girls, Mary Pipher. Riverhead Trade, 2005.

You Just Don't Understand: Men and Women in Conversation, Deborah Tannen. William Morrow Paperbacks, 2007.

Parenting

Parenting from the Heart: How to Stay Connected with Your Child in a Disconnected World, Ron Taffel & Melinda Blau. Da Capo Press, 2002.

Parenting from the Inside Out, Daniel Siegel & Mary Hartzell. Tarcher, 2004.

Raising an Emotionally Intelligent Child: The Heart of Parenting, John Gottman & Joan Declaire. Simon & Schuster, 1998.

Take Back Your Kids: Confident Parenting in Turbulent Times, William Doherty. Sorin Books, 2000.

Teach Your Children Well: Parenting for Authentic Success, Madeline Levine. Harper, 2012.

The Science of Parenting, Margot Sunderland. DK Publishing, 2008.

Social Challenges

Bowling Alone: The Collapse and Revival of American Community, Robert D. Putnam. Touchstone Books, 2001.

Loneliness: Human Nature and the Need for Social Connection, John T. Cacioppo & William Patrick. W.W. Norton & Co., 2009.

Personal Development

Daring Greatly: How the Courage to be Vulnerable Transforms the Way We Love, Parent, and Lead, Brene Brown. Gotham, 2012.

First Things First: Coping with the Ever-Increasing Demands of the Workplace, Stephen R. Covey, A. Roger Merrill, & Rebecca A. Merrill. Simon & Schuster, 1999.

Mindfulness: An Eight-Week Plan for Finding Peace in a Frantic World, Mark Williams and Danny Penman. Rodale, 2012.

Self-Compassion: Stop Beating Yourself Up and Leave Insecurity Behind, Kristin Neff. HarperCollins, 2013.

Self-Esteem: A Proven Program of Techniques for Assessing, Improving, and Maintaining Your Self-Esteem, Patrick Fanning & Matthew McKay. New Harbinger, 2000.

The Dance of Anger: A Woman's Guide to Changing the Patterns of Intimate Relationships, 20th Edition, Harriet Lerner, Perennial Currents, 2005.

The Gifts of Imperfection: Let Go of Who You Think You are Supposed to Be and Embrace Who You Are, Brene Brown. Hazelden, 2010.

The Happiness Trap: How to Stop Struggling and Start Living, Russ Harris. Trumpeter, 2008.

The Myths of Happiness: What Should Make You Happy, but Doesn't. What Shouldn't Make You Happy, but Does, Sonja Lyubomirsky. Penguin Press, 2013.

The Relaxation and Stress Reduction Workbook, Martha Davis, Elizabeth Eshelman, & Matthew McKay. New Harbinger, 2008.

The Type E* Woman: How to Overcome the Stress of being Everything to Everybody, Harriet Braiker. Backinprint.com, 2002.

When I Say No, I Feel Guilty, Manuel J. Smith. Bantam, 1985.

Why Zebras Don't Get Ulcers, Robert Sapolsky. Holt, 2004.

About Poonam Sharma, Ph.D.

 I have been practicing as a licensed psychologist in San Antonio, Texas since 1995, with a Ph.D. in counseling psychology from The University of Texas at Austin. I am also on the clinical adjunct faculty of The University of Texas Health Science Center in San Antonio.

My focus is on supporting the well-being of individuals by tapping into their strengths and helping them adapt to life changes. Over the years, I have helped thousands of women get unstuck, gain clarity, and take action to improve every aspect of their lives, including their health, relationships, career, and parenting. Since one of my practice specialties is infertility, I regularly work with professional women, many of whom have delayed building their family in order to pursue their career. As a result, I am intimately familiar with the challenges modern women face in juggling multiple roles and navigating the tremendous pressures of contemporary life. I am married and have two children, so I understand the demands of being a working woman with a very full life!

I am passionate about making the rich information and tools from my profession accessible to anyone interested in moving toward greater emotional, psychological, and physical health. I am confident that by implementing the strategies outlined in this book, you can dramatically increase your odds of a strong and healthy marriage.

Please visit www.StrongWomenStrongLove.com for more resources to strengthen both you and your marriage.

Made in the USA
San Bernardino, CA
05 August 2014